"Never Let a C

Winston Churchill immortaliz̶e̶ ... ...g..., g.v..ai ieaders to seize the moment and rebuild better than ever in the aftermath of World War II.

The savviest CEO's, entrepreneurs and professionals also recognize that a crisis is not to be wasted—that it is not a time to duck, pivot or limit your losses, but rather an unparalleled opening to rethink, reexamine and reimagine your business or career.

Necessity is the mother of reinvention.

Whether caused by external events, the actions of other people, or our own miscalculations, a crisis can provide an exceptional opportunity to come back wiser, stronger, and better positioned than before.

But how do you find the breakthrough ideas you need to get started? Transform your ideas into actionable plans? Or turn your plans into reality?

Crucial Creativity provides solid answers—not a series of theories, bromides, or platitudes, but a real world strategy that has been proven to work in the trenches of crisis, and can be implemented in your own business or career.

In the pages of this book, you will read about, and hear directly from people whose livelihoods and futures were imperiled by what seemed, at the moment, like insurmountable odds.

Some had businesses that were struck by circumstances beyond their control; some were forced to abandon career tracks or business plans that didn't pan out; some were fired from jobs or elected positions; others burned out, lost their customer base, or were betrayed by trusted colleagues.

In every instance, they found a way to leverage the strategy you'll discover in this book to create a fresh and prosperous tomorrow.

About the Author

MARK S. WALTON is a Peabody award-winning journalist, Fortune 100 management consultant, and Chairman of the Center for Leadership Communication, a global executive development enterprise with a focus on leadership and exceptional achievement in life, work and business.

Praise for *Crucial Creativity*

Great and enormously helpful! Mark Walton shows us that the shape of a crisis may be novel, but the secrets to surviving and thriving through it are not. In *Crucial Creativity*, he looks to companies and individuals who have overcome calamities in the past, and applies their strategies to today and tomorrow.

—**Barbara Bradley Hagerty**, New York Times bestselling author of *Fingerprints of God*, and contributing editor at *The Atlantic*

If you're ready to turn a crisis into a business opportunity, this book is for you. Lucidly written and filled with inspiring examples and practical insights, Mark Walton's *Crucial Creativity* can help you reinvent your organization or career to meet the moment with verve and success.

—**William Ury, Ph.D.**, international bestselling co-author, *Getting to Yes*, and co-founder, Harvard Negotiation Program

In this timely new book, Mark Walton delivers clear, innovative strategies to help us successfully recover from staggering career and business setbacks with fresh confidence and wisdom.

—**Kerry Hannon**, career columnist for the *New York Times* and AARP Magazine, and author of *Never Too Old to Get Rich: The Entrepreneur's Guide to Starting a Business at Midlife*

Mark Walton is one of our most perceptive thinkers on the importance of creativity in career and business transitions. In *Crucial Creativity*, he delivers thoughtful answers to what may be the most timely and important question yet: How do you reinvent yourself in a crisis economy?

—**Mark Miller**, Reuters columnist, *New York Times* contributor, and publisher of RetirementRevised.com

A powerful book! A beautiful blend of strategy and storytelling that will be an invaluable companion to anyone working on a business or career reinvention or even a mindset shift.

—**Marci Alboher**, VP Encore.org and author of the *Encore Career Handbook: How to Make a Living and a Difference in the Second Half of Life*

Also by Mark S. Walton

Generating Buy-In
Mastering the Language of Leadership

Boundless Potential
Transform Your Brain, Unleash Your Talents,
Reinvent Your Work in Midlife and Beyond

CRUCIAL CREATIVITY

Never Let a Crisis Crash Your Business or Career

MARK S. WALTON

profit research inc.
Established 1958 · New York

Copyright © 2020 by Mark S. Walton

All rights reserved. No part of this publication may be reproduced, distributed or transmitted in any form or by any means, including photocopying, recording, or other electronic or mechanical methods, without the prior written permission of the publisher, except in the case of brief quotations embodied in critical reviews and certain other noncommercial uses permitted by copyright law. For permission requests, please email the publisher at profitresearch@earthlink.net

Published by Profit Research Inc.

Book Design by Tracy Atkins

Crucial Creativity / Mark S. Walton — 1st ed.

ISBN:

Hardcover: 978-1-7360094-0-6
Trade Paperback: 978-1-7360094-1-3
eBook: 978-1-7360094-2-0

*To Jane, who has had my
back through every crisis*

Contents

Foreword by Mark Miller

Part One
When Crisis Strikes

Chapter 1   **The Mother of Reinvention**   7

Chapter 2   **Walt's Magic Formula**   15
Business Crisis: Walt Disney

Chapter 3   **Back to the Future**   29
Business & Career Crisis: Jack Conte

Chapter 4   **What if I'm Not The Creative Type?**   39

Part Two
Creativity in Three Acts

Chapter 5   **Observation**   49
Where Ideas Are Found

Chapter 6   **Imagineering**   67
How Creativity Takes Shape

Chapter 7   **Actualization**   85
Why Love Crafts the Final Results

Chapter 8   **How Crucial Skills Appear**   99
Personal & Career Crises: Rita K. Spina. Gil Garcetti

Part Three
Never Waste a Crisis

Chapter 9   **Meeting the Moment**   121
Creativity in the COVID-19 Crisis

Chapter 10   **Now It's Your Turn**   131
Creating Your Framework for Action

Endnotes
Acknowledgments
About the Author

Foreword

By Mark Miller
Reuters columnist, *New York Times* contributor
and publisher of RetirementRevised.com

I first met Mark Walton more than a decade ago at a conference that was focused on career reinvention with a social cause in mind, often characterized as the pursuit of 'purpose and a paycheck.'

We struck up a conversation over dinner and quickly bonded — not only due to our shared background in journalism, but also our mutual fascination with the question: how can people find a path to transforming their lives when the need arises?

This has long been a matter of importance to us both.

Several years before we met, I shifted career gears when full time work as a newspaper editor and writer became impossible as the industry consolidated and shrank. I made a leap to a new career as an independent journalist and publisher, specializing in retirement finance and aging, just as the baby boom generation began hungering for credible information on these topics.

After more than a decade as a network TV correspondent covering politics and business, Mark transitioned into the field of executive education — launching an enterprise that taught forward-looking personal and organizational leadership skills to graduate business students, as well as government, military and corporate managers.

When the great recession of 2008-9 began to derail the career and financial plans of many of his students and corporate clients, he responded by authoring a book entitled *Boundless Potential*, which explored the role of neuroscience and personal growth in career changes of many kinds.

This groundbreaking project garnered significant media attention and became the focus of a nationwide PBS Television special.

As I write this foreword to *Crucial Creativity*, Mark's subsequent book, the need for business and career reinvention has taken on new urgency, as the COVID-19 pandemic scrambles our ways of living, working and doing business, perhaps permanently.

In the U.S. alone, an estimated one in every seven small businesses has shut down; simultaneously, a bankruptcy boom has struck major American brands, including the Hertz Corporation, Frontier Communications, J.C. Penney, Lord & Taylor, Neiman Marcus, Ruby Tuesday, California Pizza Kitchen and the nutrition chain GNC.

To date, tens of millions of Americans have lost their jobs, and millions more who were temporarily furloughed may find themselves among the long-term unemployed, as formidable companies in the airline, hotel, entertainment, insurance, and other industries are forced to initiate additional layoffs.

With any significant recovery expected to take years, businesses of all sizes and individuals in many fields will need to get creative quickly—especially people in midcareer or beyond—the kind of people I write about all the time.

Evidence is growing that we're facing a huge wave of premature, unplanned retirements due to job loss; depending on your age, there might not be sufficient years to recover and get back on the path to a secure future.

Figuring out how to generate business, career or retirement income can seem daunting in such uncertain times, but in *Crucial Creativity* Mark helps guide us through the fog.

Bringing his award-winning journalistic skills to the fore, he tells the stories of business owners, corporate leaders and career professionals who developed the ability to see possibility in chaos, and then moved forward to unanticipated success by leveraging the creative strategy you will discover in this book.

The examples he shares include lesser-known accounts of legendary creators like Walt Disney and Steve Jobs, as well as those of everyday people who, in the throes of crisis, discovered creative abilities that they never knew they possessed.

And this last point reflects one of the crucial secrets revealed in the pages ahead: even if you've never been a prolific creator, you nonetheless retain the innate ability to become highly inventive at any stage of your career or life.

Mark's step-by-step analysis shows us that creative achievement is, in actuality, a deliberate practice, or series of actions, which we can learn and put into action, no matter our background or objectives. Surprisingly, this process begins with looking and listening for unexpected opportunities—and recognizing that a great idea might just be staring you in the face.

The way I see it, there could not be a better book than *Crucial Creativity* for the crises and challenging times that inevitably come our way.

PART ONE

When Crisis Strikes

CHAPTER ONE

The Mother of Reinvention

When the COVID-19 pandemic began shutting down Los Angeles in March of 2020, Drew Dalzell's business, Diablo Sound, was struck early and hard.

He recounted the dizzying speed at which his troubles converged, in an interview with the program *Marketplace* on National Public Radio:

> *There was one day it all just snowballed. There was cancellation, after cancellation, after cancellation, and we lost almost all of our bookings in one 48-hour period.*
>
> *It was like watching 20 years of building this career just evaporate around me. You know, that's devastating.*

Before the coronavirus crisis, Drew's company designed and ran audio systems for concerts, theme parks, theaters and public festivals. His major clients included Universal Pictures, Warner Brothers Studios, and Rodeo Drive in Beverly Hills.

Now, with the very notion of public gatherings in doubt, Drew had no choice but to lay off the employees he'd so carefully trained over the years—a decision he considered gut wrenching, but unavoidable.

> *If people can't gather in groups, there's no work for us. I mean it's gonna be the same situation as a coal miner when the mine shuts down.*
>
> *Intellectually, I know this is way beyond my control, but it's hard to not feel what I feel. I'm the one who decided to do this crazy thing and run a business. And a whole bunch of people signed on to come along with me. My job is to keep that going. They all did great work and yet they don't get to keep going, and so I feel like I didn't do my piece of the job.*

Drew told NPR correspondent Reema Khrais that he was trying to think up ways to pivot, or temporarily refocus his company.

But as yet, aside from raising cash to pay his mortgage, and applying for government disaster loans, the only plan he had devised was to wait to see when—or whether—the entertainment industry on which his business relied, would bounce back.

He explained his thinking this way:

> *You try to solve today's problems, you try to look as far forward as you can, and make sure you're ready to react.*

Will such an approach—being ready to react to whatever tomorrow brings—save Drew from the crisis he faces?

Perhaps.

But wouldn't it be wiser to *creatively meet the moment*, rather than hoping that things will change?

As living creatures, this choice has been ours to make for many thousands of years.

Rising to Meet the Moment

It took more than twenty centuries for the rest of us to comprehend why Plato, the ancient Greek philosopher, was right on target in 380 B.C. when he coined the phrase:

'Necessity is the Mother of Invention'

What Plato observed was that, faced with a threatening situation, people tend to react in one of two ways: either we run away from it, or we attempt to tackle it head on.

Come the early 1920's, physiologists and psychologists who were similarly intrigued by this phenomenon gave it a name — the 'fight or flight' or 'acute stress response.'

In studying the reactions of humans and other animals, they found a clear-cut pattern: on detection of a serious threat, our brains and bodies become unusually primed, through an infusion of stress hormones, to either hastily flee for perceived safety, or focus intensely on the crisis before us.

Here's what else they discovered:

If we choose to move forward, rather than delay or flee when crisis strikes, this hormone cocktail uniquely empowers us to think and act more creatively than in ordinary times.

A half century or more later, experts in the burgeoning field of organizational behavior began to document that this is demonstrably so, not only for individuals but for teams and entire companies as well.

Jay Rao, professor of innovation at Babson College, explains:

> *In good times, companies get fat, dumb, and happy when it comes to innovation.*
>
> *In a crisis, we make fewer mistakes in the choice of the problem, and we do a much better job about picking solutions.*
>
> *Innovation and creativity love crises and constraints.*

Put another way: when crisis strikes, the necessity for a solution can become the wellspring — the mother — of reinvention.

Never Waste a Crisis

Much in the way an old growth forest inferno fertilizes the soil and makes space for regeneration, a business or career crisis lays waste to the status quo and opens the way for new ideas and possibilities.

In the wake of the 2008 financial crisis, for example, venerable business models were shaken to their core, while the seeds of dozens of new multi-billion dollar companies were sown, among them: Instagram, Uber, Airbnb, Dropbox, and more.

As with other crises, writes Daniel Priestly, CEO of Dent Global:

> *Recessions can lead to reinventions.*
>
> *Companies that try to stay the same get chewed up and spat out, whereas companies that reinvent themselves do well. In many cases, small nimble businesses become the bright sparks that fly high after a recession.*

Will you cling to how your business did before, or will you use this time to transform into an even better version of your mission and values?

A High Level of Urgency

During the same time period—Spring of 2020—in which Los Angeles sound studio entrepreneur Drew Diablo watched his business evaporate in the face of the coronavirus crisis, across the country in western North Carolina, Blue Star Camp owner Seth Herschthal could see the writing on the wall.

How, he wondered, can you possibly operate a summer sleepaway camp where children and counselors live, share, eat and play in close quarters, when there's a highly contagious, potentially deadly virus, on the loose?

Seth told me:

> *It was urgent, a very high level of urgency. I think everybody got it. As with other industries, we were facing an existential crisis. The way we lived and operated were potentially never going to come back.*

After consulting with his leadership team, Seth made a crucial decision:

> *We couldn't wait to see what happens. When so much is up in the air and so much is unsettled and unknown, I think for any business, any organization, the way to survive, and then once again be in a position to thrive, is to be the one with your surfboard ready, and be the first one on that wave.*
>
> *You might wipe out, but it's framing the narrative, setting the parameters of the conversation.*

What are summer camps going to look like? Not just this summer but moving forward? How do we reimagine, rethink, reinvent, who we are and what to do?

When the summer of 2020 arrived, more than 80% of U.S. summer sleepaway camps remained shuttered in the face of the COVID-19 crisis, at a revenue loss of some $16-billion to the camping industry.

Seth, however, not only opened his camp's gates, but after holding a virus-free month long session for 350 campers aged 6 to 16, expanded his business model to include the launch of a brand new enterprise: a customized summer camp for entire families, featuring private cabins, secluded meals, and tailored outdoor activities led by specially-trained counselors to assure a safe, adventurous and memorable escape from home.

For Seth and his team this was more than a temporary pivot—it was a chance to exercise their imaginations, stretch their skills and abilities, and position themselves on a glide path to long term resilience and success.

I knew we would have to evolve or decay and the pandemic forced us, pushed us, to be creative in ways we never had before.

The family camp we did was unbelievable, with overwhelming positive feedback from all the participating families.

As a result, I think we are very well positioned to continue riding that wave, while also exploring other potential ways to grow the overall business model.

A Strategy for Reinvention

"Tough times have often benefited those with a mindset to see opportunities where others see chaos and confusion," entrepreneurship educator Sara Cochran told the *New York Times* in the depths of the coronavirus crisis.

As with all major business or career challenges, of course, moving from mindset to creative action requires a solid, practical strategy.

This book will provide you with precisely that—not a series of theories, bromides or platitudes, but a time-tested formula that has been proven to work in the fog of crisis, and can be implemented in your own business or career.

In the pages ahead, you will read about, and hear directly from people whose livelihoods and futures were imperiled by what seemed, at the time, like insurmountable odds.

Some had businesses that were struck by circumstances beyond their control; some were forced to abandon career tracks or business plans that didn't pan out; some were fired from jobs or elected positions; others burned out, lost their customer base, or were betrayed by trusted colleagues.

A number of the people whose stories we'll explore are highly accomplished individuals whose names you will instantly recognize; others are people you've likely never heard of.

In every instance, they found a way to leverage the strategy that you'll learn in this book, to create a fresh and prosperous future— one that met their individual needs as well as the evolving demands of the marketplace.

How did they accomplish this?

What can be learned from their experiences?

How does the strategy they used actually work, and how can you leverage it for yourself?

The answers will shortly become apparent.

After years of researching inventive achievement, writer Jonathan Lehrer concluded:

> *Every creative journey begins with a problem. It starts with a feeling of frustration, the dull ache of not being able to find the answer. We have worked hard, but we've hit the wall. We have no idea what to do next.*

Soon, you will know exactly what to do.

And as you continue reading, you will not only discover, but begin to personally navigate the path from the doldrums of crisis, into a new and crucial dimension of creativity.

CHAPTER TWO

Walt's Magic Formula

When you walk through the gates of Disneyland in California, Walt Disney World in Florida, or any of the dozen Disney theme parks anywhere in the world, no matter your age, it's nearly impossible to wear a frown.

The corners of your mouth automatically curl upward as you stroll past the sign that reads *'To All Who Come to this Happy Place...Welcome,'* or as you amble past the horse drawn streetcars, cross the moat to Sleeping Beauty Castle and, from there, enter the kingdom of Donald Duck and Mickey Mouse.

What most visitors don't know is that all of this happiness came out of a crisis.

It was born during a frightening period, as Walt Disney himself described it, "when the business fortunes of my brother Roy and myself were at the lowest ebb, and disaster seemed right around the corner."

Another thing few people recognize is that Walt averted that disaster with a creative strategy—a formula that he first began developing in childhood.

Where Walt Found the Magic

A saunter down 'Main Street USA,' the main thoroughfare in any Disney park is, in actuality, a tour of a nearly exact replica of Kansas Avenue in Marceline, Missouri, the little town where Walt grew up.

After he moved away, Marceline residents crafted a town motto to reflect the special nature of their rural hamlet.

It read simply: "Where Walt found the Magic."

Today, more than a century later, little remains of the massive cotton tree under which Walt spent hours alone, immersed in "belly button adventures," while lying on his stomach observing "the bugs, animals and birds, and listening to the sounds of the wind."

He didn't merely notice what was around him — over time, as children do, he began imagining that these creatures were his friends, and imbuing them, in his mind's eye, with human characteristics: names, personalities, voices.

It was under his favorite 'dreaming tree,' while his father and older brothers worked the family farm, that Walt began crayoning, on a 5-cent paper tablet, the kinds of characters that would later make him famous.

The more he drew, the more he fell in love with the process of inventing his new animal-like playmates. He later told a neighbor: "I drew whatever I saw. I could always count on rabbits and squirrels and field mice. And on a good day, sometimes Bambi came by."

Over time, he found that a retired physician named "Doc Sherwood" would actually pay him for the funny little drawings he made.

But he discovered much more than that.

Because it was in this happenstantial way that 6-year-old Walt first began to learn, and develop, the 'magic' formula with which he would build, and later rescue his career and business, when America's economy crashed.

> *First, observe the world around you for raw ideas and inspiration.*
>
> *Second, imagine ways to turn what you observe into something new.*
>
> *Third, use skills that you love to make what you imagine real.*

As we'll see throughout this book, these three actions not only changed the course of Walt Disney's career, but have long been the methodology employed by achievers of many kinds who face seemingly insurmountable problems, setbacks and failures when crisis strikes.

No matter how crucial the challenges you encounter, it's a strategy that can work for you, too.

The Three Acts of Crucial Creativity

OBSERVE — Explore what currently exists for ideas, opportunities, information and inspiration.

IMAGINEER — Imagine ways to transform your observations into solutions, innovations or inventions that meet the needs of the marketplace.

ACTUALIZE — Apply skills and abilities that you love to use to turn what you've imagined into reality.

Walt Disney, who personally invented the term *Imagineering*, became an undisputed master of this creative formula.

He was such an advocate, in fact, that he frequently came to Disney corporate offices dressed up to play the part of someone engaged in each of the three actions it encompasses.

Following one such visit, a Disney animator famously joked: "there were actually three different Walts—you never knew which one was coming to your meeting!"

Forever the entertainer, Walt deeply enjoyed these role playing exercises.

But the strategy he sought to convey was no laughing matter.

Without it, Walt could never have endured the failures, or surmounted the setbacks that came his way, while launching one of the world's most admired and enduring brands.

Let's see how this came about.

A Crisis of Betrayal

In the early 1920's, a nearly-broke Walt Disney left behind a string of disappointing flops as a young Kansas City cartoonist, to head for Hollywood, where previously unknown actors like Charlie Chaplin and Rudolph Valentino were fast becoming matinee idols in black and white silent films.

Along with his brother, Roy, Walt set up a small production studio that generated a series of modestly-successful films featuring a real-life child actress playing onscreen with cartoon 'extras.'

In the process, Walt dreamed up what he believed was a better idea:

> *Rather than casting cartoon characters as bit players, why not feature them in leading roles?*

It was a revolutionary concept at the time, one that Universal Pictures and movie distributor Charles Mintz enthusiastically bought into, hiring Walt Disney Studios to produce movies starring a Disney-created cartoon character named "Oswald the Lucky Rabbit."

But much to their dismay, Oswald's debut was a disaster.

Universal's executives hated the Oswald character, and sent Walt back to the drawing board, where he subsequently redesigned his rabbit as a more mischievous and likable critter than when he first appeared.

This turned out to be a brilliant creative move—one that transformed the next two dozen Oswald movies into popular and profitable hits!

Walt soon discovered, however, that the coast was far from clear—Universal Pictures and Charles Mintz had executed a stealthy end run that enabled them to capture all the rewards for themselves.

How did they arrange this?

First, when they hired Walt, they locked him into a contract that guaranteed them permanent rights to anything he created while in their employ—simply put, *they*, and not he, were the owners of Walt's Oswald cartoon hero as well as every film in which he had, or ever would, appear.

Later, while Walt was fixated on making Oswald a star, they secretly hired away most of the cartoonists who helped him accomplish this.

All told, they put a headlock on Walt's future prospects in a way that would easily have brought others to their knees, perhaps never to rise again.

But, since his early days back in Marceline, Walt had known the magic formula — the three acts of creativity that can turn a crisis on its head.

And he set out to do just that.

Crucial Creativity Act One: Observation
Explore what currently exists for ideas,
opportunities, information and inspiration.

Although he'd been betrayed by Hollywood heavies, and lost the rights to his first hit movies and cartoon hero, Walt came away with a priceless observation — a lesson with which he would reinvent not only his career and Walt Disney Studios, but the entire entertainment industry:

People loved cartoon heroes, but only if they seemed human.

It was a crucial insight — generated by the failure of his initial Oswald character and subsequent turnaround success — that would ultimately become the hallmark of Walt Disney's remarkable career.

As he put it:

> *The public, and especially the children, like animals that are cute and little.*

> *Without personality, the character may do funny or interesting things, but unless people are able to identify themselves with the character, its actions will seem unreal. And without personality, a story cannot ring true.*

With this realization in front of mind, Walt, his brother Roy, and animator Ub Iwerks, who had stuck with them through the Universal Pictures debacle, embarked on a process of determining who, or what, the ideal cartoon movie star might be.

Crucial Creativity Act Two: Imagineering
Imagine ways to transform your observation into solutions, innovations or inventions that meet the needs of the marketplace.

Even as their unpaid bills mounted, the Disney team sought to free their imaginations to dream up new options: what kind of animal could they base their new hero on?

Should it be a dog, a cat, pony, or frog? Would any of these be sufficiently "cute and little?" How might they be artistically engineered to seem human?

After a series of dead ends and close calls, Walt came across a human role model—the highly popular comedic actor Charlie Chaplin, known for his adorable expressions and baggy pants.

From that moment on, he later recalled, the choice was unequivocal.

We wanted something appealing, and we thought of a tiny bit of a mouse that would have something of the wistfulness of Chaplin, a little fellow trying to do the best he could. I think we are rather indebted to Charlie Chaplin for the idea.

Born of necessity, the little fellow literally freed us of immediate worry.

It wasn't long before they gave their new mascot a name.

No doubt you guessed it by now — Mickey Mouse.

> **Crucial Creativity Act Three: Actualization**
> Apply skills and abilities that you love to use
> to turn what you've imagined into reality.

Actualizing the whimsical character they had imagined — drawing Mickey on paper, then putting him on film — was, perhaps, the easiest part of beginning to make him real.

Walt, his brother Roy, and animator Ub Iwerks were, of course, highly skilled cartoonists with deep experience and love for their work.

Early distribution, however — getting their new hero into movie theaters — was another matter. It took all the passion they could muster to overcome the obstacles they found.

First, they faced an uphill battle convincing theater owners to provide time slots for films that featured animated stars.

Next, there was the disappointing fact that, once distributed, their first two Mickey Mouse movies proved to be commercial flops.

It was a matter of bad timing: Mickey debuted in theaters in late 1928, and with the Great Depression beginning to reveal its ugliness, Americans were increasingly anxious and preoccupied.

Recognizing that an extra burst of creativity might grab people's attention, Walt's team reinvented cinema, yet again, with a film titled *Steamboat Willie*, the first ever animated cartoon to synchronize movement with music and voices—in this case, Mickey singing and whistling as he piloted a charming little boat.

It was with this roll of the dice, that Mickey's star finally began to rise.

And meteorically rise….to meet the *exact needs* of the moment, and the marketplace.

Wrote one chronicler of the times: "Mickey Mouse became the one thing people could smile about. His indomitable spirit, as well as the technological advances that Disney displayed in those first cartoons, struck a chord with movie-going audiences. People became invested in Mickey Mouse. In rooting for Mickey, audiences were cheering their own success, as well."

The worse the economy became, the more Mickey was in demand.

In 1932, Walt received a special Academy award for inventing him. In 1935, the *New York Times* declared Mickey a "national treasure."

By 1938, Mickey was credited not only with spreading joy, but for concretely assisting America's recovery, as the production of hundreds of Mickey Mouse branded products—from wrist watches, to playing cards, pencils, marmalade, breakfast cereal, table covers and bracelets—helped to reopen factories, and provide new jobs.

Walt's Magic Formula

In a time of deep crisis, Walt Disney's 'magic' creative formula made life better for millions of his fellow citizens, by bringing to life a huggable little creature with big round ears, a happy whistle, and an endless smile.

On the next page, take a moment to read over the brief schematic outlining Walt Disney's crucial steps leading to the creation of Mickey Mouse and the subsequent birth of the Disney entertainment empire.

Throughout the book, you will see additional diagrams such as this, as we continue unpacking *The Three Acts of Crucial Creativity* and you begin to contemplate how you might leverage this powerful strategy for yourself.

Walt Disney's Crucial Creativity

Crisis Faced: Betrayal by business partners and loss of crucial copyright.

OBSERVE
Walt and his team were the first movie makers to observe that audiences of all ages were drawn to cute cartoon animals with human features and personalities.

IMAGINEER
While brainstorming their cartoon hero, Walt imagined a naive, huggable mouse modeled after the 'Little Tramp' character played by Charlie Chaplin, one of Hollywood's most popular silent film stars.

ACTUALIZE
Walt and his team applied their animation and production skills to bring Mickey alive in the first movies to ever synchronize cartoon characters, voices, music and action.

OUTCOME
The creation of Mickey Mouse, soon to become the world's most recognizable character and 'chief marketing officer' for the entertainment empire that Walt Disney launched in the depths of the Great Depression.

When Walt was asked, over the years, to explain his remarkable success, he was often known to respond: "I hope we never lose sight of one thing — that it was all started by a mouse."

A mouse and a global business empire that were brought into existence during America's worst financial crisis, through the 'magic' formula that Walt stumbled on in childhood:

The Three Acts of Crucial Creativity

In the next chapter, we'll see the role that this strategy played nearly a century later, as the age of social media dawned in Silicon Valley.

CHAPTER THREE

Back to the Future

In the world of Silicon Valley startups, Jack Conte became something of a legend for turning a career and business crisis *of his own making* into a stellar social media success.

Let's track his story from the starting line:

Jack graduated from Stanford University with a unique combined degree in music, technology and science—a recipe that could easily have landed him a lucrative position in the burgeoning entertainment industry.

He wanted none of it.

As much as Jack loved composing and playing music, he was also fiercely intent on being his own boss—a successful entrepreneur.

So he devised a business plan that he believed was air tight: he would jump on, and ride the new wave of the emerging social media—YouTube, iTunes, Google and other web platforms—with the goal of attracting a fan base on which he would build his own business from the ground up.

Little did he know that, in a few short years, he'd need to rescue himself from financial calamity with the strategy we've begun to examine in this book: *The Three Acts of Crucial Creativity*.

Recalled Jack:

> *Right after graduating from Stanford, I discovered YouTube, which was then a brand new video-sharing website. I started uploading my music to the service, and that's when I first began connecting with an audience and found people who liked my music.*
>
> *I got very excited about the exposure and started heavily investing in the platform and building my audience on YouTube. Within a few years, I was making a living as a professional, full-time musician, selling MP3s and doing uploads to iTunes as well.*
>
> *At the same time, I started a band with my girlfriend, now my wife, and we started selling a lot of songs. I can remember selling 30-thousand in just one month.*
>
> *And we owned all that music because we didn't sign with a record label or anything like that. So, we could just deposit what we made directly into our personal bank account.*

But mistaking revenue—cash flow—for actual business success, would lead Jack to the brink of bankruptcy.

Over time, he began plowing the money he'd earned into increasingly elaborate music videos—scaling up his ambitions at a cost that was unrealistic and, ultimately, disastrous.

Eventually the day came, he told me, when the error of his ways hit home.

> *I was putting together this music video and had contracted with a guy to help me build a robot. And we were working together to get the robot to sing the lyrics to the song.*
>
> *I was going to Home Depot every day and buying all kinds of equipment, spending a $100-bucks here, another $150-bucks there, and really racking up charges. I spent a ton of money, maxed out a credit card, and was rapidly headed underwater.*
>
> *From past experience I knew I would post the video online and get a million views from my fans, because that's what my videos were usually attracting at the time.*
>
> *But I was simultaneously terrified, because I also knew that I'd end up earning a grand total of $150-dollars in advertising revenue when I uploaded it to YouTube.*
>
> *Why? Because no matter how many people watched it, that's all these music videos ever made.*

Six years after graduating from Stanford, at a time when most of his classmates were well into profitable careers, Jack came to realize that the business he'd thought he was growing was not only built on quicksand, but sinking deeper into crisis each day.

> *And I couldn't stomach that, I couldn't take it. I had literally given 100% of myself to this business, and I just started crying, because I was so exhausted.*
>
> *I was broke, my bank account had zero dollars, and I was screwed.*

Clearly, if he still hoped to work for himself, Jack would need to start all over again — reinvent his business from the ground up.

But, given the deep financial hole he was in, how could he pull this off?

Let's take a look.

No Room for Mistakes

Having already launched one startup, albeit a failed one, Jack had learned, the hard way, the basics of creating another: he would need to find a solid idea, transform that into a realistic plan, then turn *that* into a real world solution for the crisis he currently faced.

In retrospect, he now recognized where he'd gone wrong: he'd attempted to build his first business, not on a solid evidence-based concept, but around the notion that internet advertisers would pay big dollars for access to his online music video fans.

It was a reasonable but fatally flawed assumption.

This time around, he would have zero margin for error; from square one, he would have to get things right.

Where should he begin?

Answer: where all *successful* entrepreneurs, and creators of all kinds, first start looking for new ideas, opportunities, information and inspiration - not in their heads, but in the real world, in what already exists.

And that's precisely where Jack found the key to his future business success.

> **Crucial Creativity Act One: Observation**
> Explore what currently exists for ideas, opportunities, information and inspiration.

As a musician who had grown up, gone to college, and lived in the San Francisco Bay Area, Jack had often viewed live musical performances on KQED TV, the widely admired public television station in his area.

Like other public broadcasting stations around the country, KQED had long survived on donations from viewers and listeners who were encouraged to support the station during what are commonly called 'pledge drives.'

If you've ever watched a PBS station, or listened to National Public Radio, you're likely familiar with these. They are a bit like extended commercials wedged into regular programming, often featuring on-air personalities who solicit financial support for the station.

The many millions of dollars generated this way pay for the music, drama, news and other programs on these non-commercial outlets, and provide jobs for the people who create them.

While public broadcasting has put a new spin on it, the concept of 'patronage' is centuries old — artists like Michelangelo, scientists including Galileo and da Vinci, and composers such as Beethoven and Mozart all relied on patrons to help finance their living expenses and work.

As a student of music history, and consumer of public broadcasting, Jack was aware of this phenomenon, but had never given it much thought.

Until, he told me, sitting with an empty bank account, it occurred to him that this centuries-old concept might just provide the solution he was looking for.

And, as I was thinking about this, I remember saying to myself: 'What if I just asked my fans, what if I said, hey folks, you know I'm giving everything to my work and I know you love it. I see joy, excitement and passion in your comments about the things that I'm making, so what if I just asked you for a buck a month?'

Like KQED or National Public Radio, or any of these other membership platforms, where people pay an organization a membership fee on a monthly basis. They do this because they're so moved by what these channels are providing, they want to support them.

I remember just staring at this idea and getting really excited about it, but I didn't have the guts to call anybody, I was just too scared. So I had to say to myself out loud, I said: 'this probably isn't going to work, but it's worth trying to sketch out.'

> **Crucial Creativity Act Two: Imagineering**
> Imagine ways to transform your observations into solutions, innovations or inventions that meet the needs of the marketplace.

As Jack began envisioning how to move forward, his initial approach was to post a brief request for financial support on his personal website, as well as on each of the music videos he uploaded to YouTube or other platforms.

Receiving just a few dollars a month from some of his millions of fans, he thought, could bail him out of his current troubles and potentially kick start new money-making projects to pursue.

To his surprise, the more time he spent pondering this idea, the more his imagination conjured up something much more expansive—a new business model that might not only meet his personal objectives, but help support thousands of other creative entrepreneurs like him.

Jack recalled the moment vividly:

> *One Sunday afternoon I sat down with 14 sheets of printer paper. I was in my kitchen, sitting at my kitchen table, and I began slowly sketching the whole thing out with a pen.*
>
> *And in the process of doing this, I realized that the concept of patronage might work not just for me, not just for YouTubers, but also for journalists, podcasters, web comics, illustrators, gamers or anybody who makes what the technology industry calls content.*
>
> *Every artist or solo creative entrepreneur like me who uploaded stuff online was in the same sinking ship I was — trying to make money with this weird dance between advertiser platform and user, trying to convert attention into dollars, which is a very inefficient way to make money.*
>
> *And I thought: 'this patronage thing might work for anyone who uploads content to the web and wants to be paid for it.' That was my realization — this is not just about my own website, it's a much bigger framework for a whole lot of people.*

From that breakthrough, born in the depths of his career and business crisis, emerged a rough blueprint for a website Jack would later call *Patreon.com* — a revolutionary internet portal connecting creative professionals with financial supporters from the U.S. and around the world.

> **Crucial Creativity Act Three: Actualization**
> Apply skills and abilities that you love to use to turn what you've imagined into reality.

Jack had the idea and imagination necessary to invent the Patreon concept, but to launch it into reality he would need both Silicon Valley technical expertise and venture capital.

The first person he turned to was his ex-college roommate, Sam Yam, who had studied engineering and computer science at Stanford, was an expert at software coding, and a successful serial entrepreneur.

> *When I pitched the idea to Sam, he immediately got it. He got super excited about the idea and the first thing he said to me was, 'don't tell anyone else about this idea!' And that night, he started doing research and actually designing the whole website.*
>
> *And that's how Patreon came into existence.*

In addition to creating Patreon's website, Sam helped to secure millions in venture funding from Silicon Valley friends and contacts and, along with Jack's wife, Natalie, joined the Patreon management team.

How Did Things Turn Out?

In its first six years online, Patreon.com linked visitors to the web pages, personal videos, and unique products of more than 100-thousand creative entrepreneurs who, in turn, garnered financial support from some 3-million internet patrons.

For Jack, it was a business and career reinvention beyond anything he had imagined when his original startup crashed.

> *For the first time in history, it was now possible to be a successful, viable, creative individual who could earn money online through a membership platform, from financial patronage.*
>
> *Through Patreon, they were able to connect with thousands of people who were interested in supporting them, and helping them to run small, profitable creative enterprises.*
>
> *This started to happen in a big way, and we had the data to prove it.*

Oh, by the way: soon after Patreon was launched, on top of his salary as Patreon CEO, Jack began earning up to $5000 from supportive fans for each new music video he personally posted on the site — more than 30 times what he had previously made.

On the next page, read over the brief schematic outlining the crucial acts that lead to Jack's business and career reinvention.

And when you have a moment, pay a visit to www.patreon.com to see how Jack's creation has evolved since then.

Jack Conte's Crucial Creativity

Crisis Faced: Failure of an internet-based career and business model.

OBSERVE — Jack observed that public broadcasting TV and radio stations have long relied on the financial support of their members, or patrons, to survive and thrive.

IMAGINEER — Jack imagined and sketched out rough blueprints for an internet platform that would connect creative individuals with patrons who admired and might support their work.

ACTUALIZE — Jack used his passion and expertise as an internet-savvy creator, while his friend, Sam Yam, applied his computer and entepreneurial skills to make what Jack had imagined real.

OUTCOME
Patreon.com, an internet crowdfunding platform that, by the year 2020, had provided 200-thousand creators with over $1-billion in support from some 6-million patrons from the U.S. and around the world.

CHAPTER FOUR

What if I'm Not The Creative Type?

If you're someone who has come to believe, or has been told, that you're not 'naturally creative,' how do you successfully reinvent a career or business faced with a crisis—whether one of your own making, or a crisis generated by events outside your control?

Here's what you need to know:

> *First of all, by nature, you're no less creative than anyone else, including some of the world's greatest creative achievers.*
>
> *Secondly, even if you've never created anything of consequence, or haven't done so for quite some time, you harbor the ability to become highly creative at any time in your life.*

Don't take my word for it.

Better, listen to Milton Glaser, one of America's most celebrated graphic designers, and the creator of the iconic "I ♥ NY" logo, who explains it this way:

> *There's no such thing as a creative type. As if creative people can just show up and make stuff....as if it were that easy!*
>
> *It's about taking an idea in your head, and transforming it into something real.*
>
> *I think people need to be reminded that creativity is a verb!*

Simply put, creativity results from taking certain actions, not from being a certain kind of person.

Creativity is *not* a mystery to be solved, character trait, spontaneous occurrence, or outpouring of unique talents, despite what many of us may have been told.

Creativity is a deliberate practice—a series of actions.

Further, the inherent ability to effectively leverage these actions— to mentally generate, and physically actualize solutions, innovations and inventions—was built into your genes at birth.

Famed neurobiologist Robert Sapolsky explains:

> *If you find yourself sitting close to a chimpanzee, staring face to face and making sustained eye contact, something interesting happens, something that is alternately moving, bewildering, and kind of creepy. When you gaze at this beast, you suddenly realize that the face gazing back is that of a conscious individual, who is recognizably kin.*

And no wonder: by decoding the chimpanzee genome in recent years, researchers have proven that chimps share an overwhelming percentage of our DNA—in fact, some scientists believe it may be close to 98%.

Like us, chimps experience feelings, ranging from exhilaration to depression and anger; they have the ability to acquire and teach new skills to their children; they lead complex social lives, play political games and, while often cooperative and altruistic, have been known to betray and even kill each other.

They have surprisingly high IQ's and, sometimes, amazing brain powers, including nearly photographic memories.

But they live strictly in the here and now—they can't imagine scenarios, make plans, or design their tomorrows.

They can't dream up ideas or turn them into material reality.

Of all the earth's living creatures, only you and I, homo sapiens, can do this.

Locating Your Inherent Creativity

We can't locate our inborn creativity with a scalpel or a CT scan, but we can easily recall it when we think back to our childhood.

In our early years, it was extraordinarily active.

It was working through us when we made up games in the backyard or put on shows in the living room.

It was inspiring us when we tried on our parents' eyeglasses or jewelry, dressed up in costumes, turned mud into pies, cardboard boxes into hideaways, pillows into forts, sheets into tents, or sand into castles.

Erik Erickson, the Pulitzer prize winning psychologist, tells us:

> *You see a child at play, and it is like seeing an artist paint, for in play a child says things without uttering a word. You see how he solves his problems. You can also see what's wrong. Young children, especially, have enormous creativity.*

But one day, in too many cases, our innate creativity was driven underground.

Teachers or parents began telling us, no doubt with good intentions, that there was only one correct answer to every problem; that test scores mattered more than day dreaming; text books and instructional videos were more important than observation, experimentation or discovery.

At first, some of us may have resisted, only to find ourselves labeled stubborn or uncooperative; eventually, if we managed to suppress our creativity long enough, we may have forgotten that it ever existed.

Sherwin B. Nuland, the acclaimed surgeon and National Book Award winning author, once lamented how commonly this occurs:

> *You come out of college, and you begin working for some big company or something, and everything that has come before is laid aside. You become an executive, a stockbroker, a doctor, a lawyer, or whatever, and all of your energies are devoted to that. And you become something less than your full potential.*

But while our creative potential may go into hibernation, neuroscientists assure us that it never disappears—it's a genetic gift that remains within all of us, waiting to be leveraged, from cradle to grave.

Creative Achievers Thrive in Crisis

If, in fact, there is a principal difference between highly creative achievers and the rest of us, it is their resolute determination to practice the verbs—to take the strategic actions necessary to consistently produce creative ideas, solutions or products.

They do this despite the intrinsic uncertainties, obstacles, setbacks, and the chronic risk of failure embodied in every creative venture.

Notes author Jonah Lehrer:

> *When we tell one another stories about creativity, we tend to leave out this part of the creative process. Because failures contradict the romantic nature of events, we forget all about them. Instead we skip straight to the breakthroughs. We tell happy endings first.*
>
> *The danger of this narrative is that the act of being stumped is an essential part of the creative process. Before we can find the answer, we must be immersed in disappointment, convinced that the solution is beyond our reach - we need to have wrestled with the problem and lost.*

Thus, in a very concrete sense, creative professionals such as entrepreneurs, filmmakers, scientists, inventors, chefs, artists, designers, writers, composers and the like, operate in a continual state of career and business crisis.

They have no choice but to steadfastly meet the needs of the moment—satisfy or exceed the yearnings of the marketplace, lest their reputations and future prospects suffer, perhaps irrecoverably.

As award-winning actor and screenwriter Alan Bennet explains: "there is no next time, no time-outs, no second chances…it's now or never" for highly accomplished creators.

In an inescapable way, they live, breathe, and rely deeply on *The Three Acts of Crucial Creativity* each and every working day.

This makes them ideal mentors—outstanding role models—for those of us who seek to invent, or reinvent, our own businesses or careers, especially when crisis strikes.

Mastering the Process

To this point in the book, through the stories of Walt Disney and Jack Conte's reinventions, we've skimmed the surface of the crucial creativity process.

In the next section, with the goal of infusing your mental DNA with this strategy, we'll take a deeper dive into its inner workings, with some of the world's most adept practitioners as our guides.

While you absorb the lessons ahead, it's vital to understand that:

Even if you work in an entirely different field, even if the challenges you face bear no resemblance to theirs, their methodology for turning a crisis on its head — for transforming failures and setbacks into opportunities — can be leveraged to create solutions, innovations and inventions in your own business or career.

Therefore, discovering first-hand how masters of crucial creativity operate, will take you a step closer to mastering their best practices.

In the chapters to come, we'll unpack their modus operandi one act at a time.

Observation
Where Ideas Are Found

We'll see the indispensable role that observation played in the creative accomplishments of super creators like fashion entrepreneur Eileen Fisher, acclaimed chef and restauranteur Davide Oldani, actor/director Bradley Cooper, as well as legendary creators Paul McCartney, Bob Dylan and more.

Imagineering
How Creativity Takes Shape

We'll discover how imagination really works through the words and experiences of Albert Einstein, Oscar-winning movie maker Steven Spielberg, renowned artist Salvador Dali, inventor Nickola Tesla, and Mary Shelley, the novelist who created Frankenstein.

Actualization
Why Love Crafts the Final Result

We'll learn from Steve Jobs, Tony award winning producer Jordan Roth, pioneering psychologist Mihaly Csikszentmihalyi and others, how to use our personal skills and abilities, including those we loved as kids, have applied at work, or might yet develop, to transform what we imagine into reality.

In addition, as we navigate these topics, each chapter ahead will provide you with a customized exercise designed to wrap your thoughts and actions around the levers and dials of the crucial creativity process, as you prepare to put it to work for yourself.

So let's dive in.

PART TWO

Creativity in Three Acts

CHAPTER FIVE

Observation

Where Ideas Are Found

Eileen Fisher's crisis struck early, and rolled through her career like a slow-moving locomotive crushing everything on its tracks.

If not for an unexpected observation while this was occurring, she might never have become one of the world's most successful fashion gurus or built the global brand that bears her name.

> **Observation is the first act in the practice of crucial creativity.**
> It's how creative achievers discover clues to new
> beginnings and breakthroughs in good times and bad.

Eileen grew up in the 1950's in Des Plaines, Illinois, often called "Hometown U.S.A." because the nation's first McDonald's restaurant was located here.

At the Catholic high school she attended students wore uniforms —burgundy jumpers and white blouses—an outfit that Eileen adored, because it made it simple for her to dress quickly each morning and dash out the door.

Ironically, this would become a serious strike against her, when, after majoring in home economics in college, she moved to Manhattan with dreams of becoming a successful interior designer.

Her uptown ambitions soon turned to ash.

Looking back, she explained why.

> *I was trying to work as a designer and trying to look like a designer, but I was struggling to put myself together — it was just overwhelming for me.*
>
> *I needed to look good, but I didn't want to think about it too much. In New York City, however, that didn't work.*

Not only did she flop at dressing the part of an interior designer, she wasn't much of a people person, and struggled while trying to sell her ideas to potential clients.

Add it all up, and Eileen's focus on interior design proved to be a total disaster — she ended up barely supporting herself by waiting tables, and piecing together small jobs designing calendars and greeting cards.

While doing this, however, she ran into a big time graphic designer at a Kinko's copy shop who had clients in Japan, and asked Eileen to travel with him there to help out with one of his advertising projects.

That's how it came about—the accidental observation that would transform her from a struggling 30-something with an uncertain future, into *the* Eileen Fisher—the fashion designer whose label today adorns hundreds of thousands of pieces of women's clothing in the U.S. and worldwide.

A Fateful Observation

The sighting occurred in Kyoto, the ancient Japanese capital, where real-life geishas and geisha look-alikes commonly walked the streets.

This was where Eileen saw her first kimono.

> *I got inspired. I saw it work in different ways. I saw all those little cotton kimonos and those kimono things they wear in the rice patties with little flood pants.*
>
> *There were the colors, and the shape, and that was the same shape for like a thousand years in Japan. It was the only shape they wore.*
>
> *I was fascinated by the idea that one design, one shape, could transcend time, and be made new just by different patterns and colors.*
>
> *I stored that idea about the kimono.*

She held the observation in her memory bank—but to what end?

On returning to New York, she continued scratching out a living through whatever graphic design gigs she could find.

Yet the image of clothes for American women, based on the kimono, wouldn't leave her alone—simple outfits, made of good fabric that made dressing up fast and easy.

Garments that you could mix and match from season to season, that were always colorful and chic—exactly what she'd always wanted for herself.

> *This idea kept haunting me, this clothing thing, the kimono.*
>
> *I was living in Tribeca and had artist friends and designer friends. I was dating a guy who was a sculptor. He was designing jewelry and had taken a booth at a boutique show, where owners of small clothing stores from around the country came to New York to buy clothes and accessories from small designers.*
>
> *He took me to the show and I remember looking around and going, 'I could do this.' I had never designed any clothes, but I could picture it, I could see clothes that I had designed on the walls.*

She could *imagine* it in her mind's eye, but how was she going to *create* it?

She had only $350 in the bank, didn't know how to draw clothing templates, and still worse, didn't know how to sew.

A Roll of the Dice

What she'd envisioned started to seem like a silly pipe dream when, suddenly, an invitation appeared: her sculptor friend asked her to take over his booth at the next boutique show, which was only three weeks away.

So she scrambled and improvised—what other option was there?

With what little money she had to work with, she went out and purchased clothes that were similar to what she had in mind — items that, with nips and tucks, might bring her closer to her mental blueprint.

Next, she found a seamstress who was willing to follow her quirky instructions.

> *And I said to Gail, the woman who was making the patterns: 'it's kind of like this, but the neck is more like that, and it's a little longer, or it's a little shorter, it's a little wider, it's got a long sleeve or a shorter sleeve or something like that.'*
>
> *Gail sewed the clothes — there were four garments made of linen — and I took them to the boutique show and hung them up. I remember being terrified standing there and waiting for what people would say.*
>
> *But everyone was kind, maybe because I was quiet and shy.*
>
> *Eight stores made small orders totaling $3,000, and several buyers even sat down with me and said: 'We like your shapes, but try a different fabric,' or 'Your colors are not quite in sync with what's in fashion now.'*
>
> *I listened, made adjustments, and for my second show, I built off the first line by adding a simple skirt, a straight dress, and a drop-waist dress, all in a French terry.*
>
> *I sold $40,000 worth of clothes and took the stack of orders to the bank to borrow money I needed to make them. People stood in line. They loved the new fabric, the styles, and the modular concept.*

That's how Eileen Fisher's $350 investment in a few pieces of store-bought clothing, and a few hours of seamstress time, eventually grew into a $400-million global clothing brand.

It all started with an unexpected observation, during a young woman's early career crisis.

Don't Buy-Into the Myth of Genius

As we'll see throughout this book, an act of observation can provide the opening for an innovative new product, scientific breakthrough, original artistic genre, new business or career plan, even a major enterprise like Eileen Fisher's.

Indeed, contrary to the conventional myth that revolutionary ideas are the products of 'special geniuses,' the world's most creative business people, scientists, musicians, writers, performers, artists and others readily admit—and often teach— that detective work is crucial to their success.

Igor Stravinsky, perhaps the most influential composer of the 20th Century, likened creative achievers to hungry animals on the prowl, during his lectures at Harvard:

> *Both go grubbing about because they yield to a compulsion to seek things out. So we grub about in expectation of our pleasure, guided by our scent, and suddenly we stumble against an unknown. It gives us a jolt, a shock and this shock impregnates our creative power.*

What are the crucial takeaways in this—the deliverables—that might matter most to you and me, when we're up against the wall in a crisis, in need of a new idea around which to reinvent a business or career?

Here are three key lessons to keep in front of mind:

Lesson #1
Stop, Look and Listen for the Unexpected

George de Mestral, the engineer who created Velcro, was hunting in the Swiss mountains, when he looked down and observed that tiny cockle-burs had attached themselves to his pants and his dog's fur.

Later, studying these carefully under a microscope, he noticed how the bur's tiny hooks had fastened onto the fabric of his trousers.

With the help of friends in the weaving business, de Mestral duplicated this "hook and loop" process, which ultimately led to the patenting of Velcro, whose brand name is derived from the French words for velvet (velour) and hook (crochet).

Writes creativity researcher Pagan Kennedy, who has documented numerous creative breakthroughs similar to de Mestral's:

> *Some inventions could only have started with a random encounter. This process is so common that we have a name for it: accidental invention.*

But be forewarned, she adds—the possibilities that may reside inside everyday encounters are only available to those who are wise enough to notice them.

> *People who feel 'lucky' tend to be especially observant, and that ability to scan their surroundings makes it easier for them to notice useful clues in their environment.*

Here are several more quick examples of observations leading to "accidental inventions," as told by Robert Kriegel, an Olympic coach and corporate consultant, in his book *If It Ain't Broke, Break It*.

> *Clarence Birdseye revolutionized the retail food industry and built a giant company because he seized on an unexpected opportunity. While on a fishing trip to Canada he noticed an Eskimo's fish frozen on ice. That observation gave him the original idea for 'frozen food,' an industry that Birdseye pioneered.*
>
> *Similarly, the Upjohn pharmaceutical company was testing Minoxidil, a crystalline solid developed for reducing high blood pressure. Volunteers reported moderate success with their blood pressure, but an unexpected side effect was that they began growing hair.*

Through a subsequent reinvention of its original formulation, Upjohn launched Rogaine, the blockbuster product that has long dominated the hair regrowth market.

Lesson #2
Great Ideas May be Right in Front of You

Davide Oldani is widely regarded as one of the most creative contemporary chefs and restauranteurs in the world.

So much so, that he's been featured in the *Harvard Business Review* for inventing a culinary business model that allows him to "offer meals at approximately one-third the price of other Michelin starred restaurants."

How did he accomplish this?

After completing his gastronomic training in Paris, London and Monaco, Davide returned to his hometown outside Milan to open D'O, a small restaurant of his own, which developed an 18-month waiting list in its first year of operation.

Not due to what he had learned abroad, in school, or in his mother's kitchen — but because of the way he reinvented Michelin star dining, based on a simple observation about the area where he grew up.

Explained Davide:

> *It's full of rice fields here, from here to Abbiategrasso, there are the rice fields. So my inspiration is very simple, because I see rice as a blank canvas on which I can write in any color at any moment of the year.*

Depending on what's fresh and in season, chef Davide may 'write' on rice with chicken and prawns, as in his universally acclaimed 'Riso Chicken and Prawn,' topped with veal jus, spicy raisins, scent of thyme and creamy carnaroli.

At other times, rice from the nearby meadows might be garnished with mussels and wild fennel, peas, almonds, or fresh local frogs.

> *The blank canvas is the rice, the color is the seasonal ingredient. Rice and frogs are already a dish, a well-defined dish. So, the nourishing base is the white part of the canvas. And the part that gives flavor is the ingredient of that season.*

Aldani's simple approach has been given a fancy name — Cucina Pop Style — by food critics and journalists, who've lavished praise on his ability to transform ordinary, often humble food, into bold and wondrous meals.

Asked about his earliest memories of cooking, Davide recalled:

> *It was gnocchi made by my mother, which I later reinvented by changing the cooking method where instead of boiling the gnocchi, I roasted them in a pan with a veil of extra virgin olive oil.*

In the domain of world class Italian cooking, Davide Oldani has reinvented just about everything—recipes, costs, and the way food is served.

"Drawing on what my homeland gives me" he said, "with the correct balance, I create my dishes."

Lesson #3
It's Okay to "Steal Like an Artist"

If creativity can be inspired by the unexpected, so too can it be sparked by observing what other creators have accomplished.

Many big name innovators have unabashedly borrowed from, improvised on, and reinvented what others have created before them, and have enthusiastically endorsed this as an invaluable technique.

Consider these remarkable musicians:

Paul McCartney, the Grammy Award winning singer and composer of many of the Beatles' megahits, as well as his own, has readily acknowledged that, at the beginning of his career, "I emulated Buddy Holly, Little Richard, Jerry Lee Lewis, Elvis. We all did."

Bob Dylan, the legendary composer, singer and Nobel Laureate, reignited his own career, at age 60, with a collection of songs aptly titled *Love and Theft*.

Rolling Stone magazine said of it: "He plundered the entire history of American music," and Dylan unhesitatingly agreed, saying: "All my songs, the styles I work in, were all developed before I was born. When I came into the world, Billie Holiday was still alive. Duke Ellington. All those old blues singers were still alive. And that was the music that was dear to me. I was never really interested in pop music."

Turning to the world of business, we could fill entire pages with examples of the ways in which companies, large and small, have observed and admired each other's creativity. In top MBA programs, professors develop case studies and devote entire courses to this topic, as it is such a crucial part of product development and marketing strategy.

Here are a few fundamental examples from American corporate history:

Retail Industry

'Does Macy's tell Gimbel's?' was a frequently-repeated half joking, half pithy commentary about the 75-year rivalry between these two iconic family-founded American department store chains. At times, it seemed that each so closely observed the other's creativity in product selection and marketing, that the popular Christmas movie, "*Miracle on 34th Street*" featured a Macy's Santa Claus steering customers to Gimbels, to buy the same or similar products for less.

Automotive

Toyota Motor Company, after researching the U.S. auto market, was the first manufacturer to begin creating, and exporting, Japanese-made cars specifically designed to attract American consumers.

Crucial Creativity

Wrote *Autoweek* Magazine about the 1959 Toyopet Crown Sedan, which was Toyota's initial export to the U.S.: "It certainly wasn't big, or fast, or luxurious, so intrepid marketers appealed to prospective buyers' pocketbooks...and thus, the little car was billed as the world's greatest automotive value."

Observing Toyota's market entry, Datsun (now Nissan) soon followed, as did Mazda and Subaru. Each continues today to keep a watchful eye on the price, size, features, safety record, fuel efficiency, and design of their competitors' new models.

Media

Ted Turner, the entrepreneur who created CNN, was the owner of a fledgling Atlanta TV station in the 1970's, when he first observed that television production companies had begun experimenting with program distribution via new-fangled communication satellites.

His decision, in 1976, to start using satellite technology to beam his small, local station to cable and satellite dish subscribers nationwide, created WTBS—America's first 'superstation.' Four years later, Turner connected satellite delivery with newly emerging cable technology, to create CNN, the world's first all-news network.

By now, I'm sure you've gotten the point: creators of all kinds make a strategic practice of observing what's already been created by others, in their search for new ideas, opportunities and inspiration to create the 'next new thing.'

But before moving on, there's a quintessential Hollywood story that I think you'll enjoy, because it so beautifully buttons this chapter up with movies, stars, songs, scripts, booze, the works.

OBSERVATION

A Star is Born, Over and Over

"It's the same story told over and over."

Sam Elliot, Oscar nominee for best supporting actor, delivered this line in the 2018 version of *A Star is Born*, starring Bradley Cooper, also the movie's director, and Lady Gaga, in her acting debut on the silver screen.

Indeed Cooper, while conceiving his personal rendition of the original film by the same name, unabashedly reported: "I just had all these images rolling around in my head."

And no wonder: *A Star is Born* is nearly as old as Hollywood itself.

In all, there have been five remakes to date, albeit that the first one came out in black and white, and under a different name.

1. What Price Hollywood? (1932) Lowell Sherman and Constance Bennett
2. A Star is Born (1937) Fredric March and Janet Gaynor
3. A Star is Born (1954) James Mason and Judy Garland
4. A Star is Born (1976) Kris Kristofferson and Barbra Streisand
5. A Star is Born (2018) Bradley Cooper and Lady Gaga

From decade to decade, director to director, screenwriter to screenwriter, star to starlet, there've been updates—sometimes big modifications in dialog, music and location, hair style and wardrobe.

But for each version, the film's new re-creators look back, for substance and inspiration, to the original film—and, in every case, the story remains the same.

Billboard Magazine's senior editor, Joe Lynch, describes it this way:

> *A talented girl with big dreams that have yet to materialize meets a famous-but-troubled artist who helps boost her career. They fall in love, and as her career ascends, his plummets thanks to addiction woes; she tries to help him, but he ends up dying.*

Every time the next reinvention of the film comes out, and audiences eat it up, film producers and reviewers are inspired to start mulling the storyline, all over again, as Turner Classic Movie host, Ben Mankiewicz, mused in *Vanity Fair*:

> *Perhaps the next version will experiment with gender or sexuality, or mix up the musical genre, or maybe it will tackle our newest by-products of fame: reality stars. Maybe the next 'A Star Is Born' is gonna be in 2027, and the cast will be all Kardashians.*

It very well could be — keep watching.

———

As we've seen, for highly accomplished creators of every kind, observation is the first act, the initial phase of a new project or undertaking.

So a note of caution is in order, for you and me, when it becomes crucial for us to reinvent our business or career:

Even under ordinary circumstances, most of us are losing our ability to be observant.

To test this out, give the following thought experiments a try:

Ask Yourself: What Would I Have Done?

On a Friday in early 2007, *The Washington Post* set up, and videotaped, an unusual live experiment at the L'Enfant Plaza metro station, one of downtown Washington's busiest passenger hubs, in the middle of morning rush hour.

The newspaper arranged for a young man wearing jeans, a long-sleeved tee shirt, and a Washington Nationals baseball cap, to position himself against a wall next to a trash basket.

According to columnist Gene Weingarten, who observed and won a Pulitzer Prize for his article on this experiment: the young man then removed a violin from a small case, placed the open case at his feet, threw in a few dollars as seed money, turned to face pedestrians as they walked by, and began to play.

Street performers in Washington aren't generally newsworthy, but this time was different: the violinist was 39-year-old Joshua Bell, "one of the finest classical musicians in the world, playing some of the most elegant music ever written on one of the most valuable violins ever made."

"Three days before he appeared at the Metro station," wrote Weingarten, "Bell had filled the house at Boston's stately Symphony Hall, where merely pretty good seats went for $100. Two weeks later, at the Music Center at Strathmore, in North Bethesda, he would play to a standing-room-only audience so respectful of his artistry that they stifled their coughs until the silence between movements".

After stationing himself in the subway station, Bell performed six classical pieces, over a period of 43 minutes, as 1,097 people passed by.

"Each passerby had a quick choice to make," Weingarten reported: "Do you stop and listen? Do you hurry past with a blend of guilt and irritation... annoyed by the unbidden demand on your time and your wallet? Do you throw in a buck, just to be polite?

Does your decision change if he's really bad? What if he's really good?"

Three minutes into the performance, after 63 people had passed by, there was a close call—a middle aged man hesitated for a split second, then kept walking. A little while later, a woman threw a dollar into Bell's violin case and quickly moved on.

"Things never got much better," Weingarten reported, "in the three-quarters of an hour that Joshua Bell played, 7 people stopped what they were doing to hang around, at least for a moment," and 20 more threw a little cash into his violin case, before scooting off.

In total, nearly 98% of people completely ignored what was happening directly in front of them. Only one demographic consistently broke the mold: "every time a child walked by, he or she tried to stop and watch."

But most people who were oblivious to Joshua Bell's music were grownups like Calvin Myint, a federal employee who the Washington Post caught up with, and interviewed a few hours after the metro station concert.

Myint, reported the newspaper: "got to the top of the escalator, turned right and headed out a door to the street. A few hours later, he had no memory that there had been a musician anywhere in sight."

"Where was he, in relation to me?" Myint asked. "About four feet away," answered the reporter. "Oh" replied Myint.

Observed the *Post:* "There was nothing wrong with Myint's hearing. He had buds in his ears. He was listening to his iPod."

Ask Yourself: Have I Tuned Out the World?

In a column headlined: *"How I Ditched My Phone and Unbroke My Brain,"* Kevin Roose, a leading *New York Times* technology reporter, documented his personal journey from 5 and 37 minutes of daily phone time, to practically none.

"I noticed that I reach for my phone every time I brush my teeth," Kevin wrote, "and for some pathological reason, I always check my email during the 3-second window between when I insert my credit card into a chip reader at the store, and when the card is accepted."

Mostly, Kevin noted, he became aware of how uncomfortable he had become with stillness and quiet, and how much he needed to intentionally practice observing his surroundings.

With the help of a friend, Kevin forced himself to take a 48-hour break, during which he didn't allow himself to use his phone or any other digital device.

This was no small feat for a technology pro—but, he reported, it was an illuminating, even life-changing experience.

Wrote Kevin: "During my morning walk to the office, I looked up at the buildings around me, spotting architectural details I'd never noticed before. On the subway, I kept my phone in my pocket and people-watched, noticing the nattily dressed man in the yellow hat, the kids with the Velcro shoes.

When a friend ran late for our lunch, I sat still and stared out the window instead of checking Twitter—I felt that something fundamental had shifted inside my brain. I still love the online world, and probably always will. But now the physical world excites me too—the one that has room for boredom, idle hands, and space for thinking.

It's an unnerving sensation, being alone with your thoughts...but for the first time in years, I'm starting to feel like a human again."

Ask Yourself: Am I Willing to Tune Back In?

Remember: of all the world's species, only human beings are born with the innate potential to create, to bring something new and original into existence.

But in order to do so, even when crisis strikes, we must nurture the inner stillness and quiet necessary to observe — to see, hear, touch and taste — the world as it currently exists.

Because only through observation can new ideas appear.

CHAPTER SIX

Imagineering

How Creativity Takes Shape

Imagine the following scenario:

> Cancer experts from around the country carry their morning coffee into a conference room deep in the heart of the famous Mayo Clinic in Rochester, Minnesota.
>
> Once the large screen is lowered into place, computer graphics summarize what is fast becoming a U.S. health care quagmire: despite advances in treatment for early stage prostate cancer, the disease is now recurring in some 200-thousand men each year.
>
> Therefore, the goal of today's meeting is to brainstorm a solution to the central problem underlying the crisis: when prostate cancer initially returns, it does so in a microscopic form that's too tiny to be located in the body with existing imaging technology.
>
> Later, when the cancer has spread enough to be seen on a scan, it's too far along to be cured.
>
> The result is a medical conundrum that has stumped even the best doctors for far too long.

> As they review the data, the attending physicians sit quietly in their ergonomic chairs, mulling over potential interventions.
>
> Some silently drum their fingertips on their desktops.
>
> Then, suddenly, one jumps to her feet: 'I think I may have it,' she says. 'It just came to me in a flash. Let's put patients on a low carbohydrate diet. There are reports that this slows recurrent cancer in mice, so why not give it a try?'
>
> Another participant, with a PhD in molecular biology, chimes in: 'Yes, another idea just popped into my mind. Let's start the diet regimen immediately after initial surgery or radiation. Maybe, that way, we can halt any recurrence in its tracks.'
>
> Over the next several hours, the giant whiteboard on the meeting room wall starts filling up with dozens of proposed solutions.
>
> Then, it's time to break for lunch, after which nothing ever results from this session.

How come?

Because, while the medical predicament described in this scenario is entirely factual, no session designed to resolve it in the way I've described, would ever be held at the Mayo Clinic or any other major medical institution.

The pervasive myth that breakthroughs in science, business or the arts suddenly appear through so-called 'creative brainstorming' is total pop hooey.

Real life solutions, innovations and inventions rarely, if ever, arrive as epiphanies or instantaneous realizations to individuals or groups.

They result from marrying human imagination with strategic thinking—a process that occurs quite naturally in an organized mind.

Walt Disney invented a term for this—he called it *Imagineering*.

Does it require some special talent or training?

Absolutely not.

As we'll see in this chapter, it's a capability that's activated by posing a simple question: *What if?*

Imagineering is the second act in the practice of crucial creativity.
It's how creative achievers generate solutions, innovations and inventions by mentally reengineering their observations.

Friedrich Wilhelm Nietzsche, the famous German philosopher and poet, described how the act of imagineering works:

> *Creators have a vested interest in our believing in the flash of revelation, the so-called inspiration, shining down from heavens as a ray of grace.*
>
> *In reality however, the imagination of the good thinker produces continuously good, mediocre or bad things, but his judgment, trained and sharpened to a fine point, rejects, selects, connects.*
>
> *All great creators and thinkers are great workers, indefatigable not only in inventing, but also in rejecting, sifting, transforming, ordering.*

Rejecting, sifting, transforming, ordering—what do these things have to do with creativity?

To find out, let's go back to the Mayo Clinic, and see what actually did happen there in the early 2000's — and how the question *What if?* led to a revolutionary shift in the way prostate cancer recurrence is treated today.

First Observation, then Imagineering

Dr. Eugene Kwon, a leading Mayo Clinic urologist and immunologist, described the problem that he and his colleagues set out to solve this way:

> *One of the greatest problems with regards to how to manage prostate cancer has been the fact that we haven't had a very good technology to pinpoint the location of cancers that recur or come back after initial treatment. And according to the data, roughly 200,000 men will fail initial treatment for prostate cancer every year.*
>
> *Historically, the way we've been able to identify the location of cancer coming back has been to use technology such as CT scan, bone scan, or MRI.*

Unfortunately, however, as we saw earlier, by the time these conventional imaging methods can reliably detect the cancer, it may be too widespread to cure.

What if, however, there was another method — something never previously imagined? A new way to locate the cancer while it's still microscopic and provide another chance for surgery or radiation to get rid of it, once and for all?

Dr. Val Lowe, a noted Mayo Clinic radiologist, joined Kwon and his team, in analyzing this question.

Drawing on their decades of clinical observation, research and experience, they postulated numerous approaches by which they might realize their goal.

They sifted through the possibilities that arose in their deliberations, modifying and transforming them, ordering and reordering them — and then threw them into the trash.

All but one.

The key observation that stuck with them was this: in order to grow and spread, prostate cancer cells hungrily soak up a vitamin-like nutrient called Choline, which is naturally present in the body.

Based on this observation, they began to ask themselves: *What If?*

> What if they could create an artificial, radioactive Choline-like substance that scans could detect?

> What if, by injecting this substance into a patient's body, they could get the recurring cancer cells to absorb it?

> What if they could then pinpoint the cancer and kill it?

Ultimately, these were the *What if's?* — the hypotheses, as Dr. Lowe characterized them — that led to their huge breakthrough in advanced prostate cancer care.

So the hypothesis is that the cancer cells are going to need Choline to divide and grow, and if we could identify those cells that were using a lot of Choline, we would be able to identify where possible cites of returning prostate cancer are.

As a result of experimenting with this approach, in 2012 the Mayo Clinic received federal approval to manufacture a new substance called C-11 Choline—a synthetic Choline with radioactive properties—and began to use it regularly, in conjunction with specially-designed PET scans, to detect how and where prostate cancer recurs.

As Dr. Lowe soon reported:

> *Sometimes when you look at these images, you'll see a couple of normal things, but even deep within the image you can see a beacon lighting up, showing us where the cancer is.*
>
> *Even on a single image of the whole body, you're essentially looking through all of the other normal structures in the body, going right to where the cancer is.*

What today seems like an 'out of the blue' medical miracle to tens of thousands of prostate cancer patients, began when a small group of doctors began posing *What if?* questions that had never previously been asked.

Because that's how the gears of imagineering begin turning.

Now, let's try out this process ourselves, in a much lower-risk situation.

Try This Imagineering Experiment

Relax for a moment while we do a brief experiment together. I think you'll enjoy doing it, and make a number of important discoveries.

The first thing to do is to roll this short phrase over in your mind a few times:

A Perfect Summer Afternoon

Try listening to yourself speak this phrase, silently or out loud. Then, just chew on it for a minute or two. There's no rush. After all, it's a perfect summer afternoon.

What do you see in your mind's eye?

Where are you on this perfect summer afternoon?

What's the weather like?

Who's there with you?

When I've done this experiment in university and corporate workshops, most people are ready to put on their shorts or bathing suits. They see themselves at the ocean, at mountain lakes, or on the golf course. Others are simply enjoying quiet time at home, in the backyard or on the front porch.

Okay, now let's add this element to your scenario:

What if you could have any three food items delivered to you?

What would make you happiest?

In the space below, or on a scrap of paper, jot them down in order of personal preference.

1.

2.

3.

Now let's address a final question:

What if you could have any three beverages?

Again, please job them down in order of preference:

1.

2.

3.

Excellent, now let's take a moment to look at what you've accomplished.

To begin with, you've imagined a location where you could happily spend a perfect summer afternoon. In your mind's eye, you were able to see it, feel what the weather was like, listen to sounds around you, and decide who you would like to have join you, or whether you'd prefer to be alone.

Then, when we proposed that you could have anything you wanted to eat and drink, you 'pulled up,' seemingly out of nowhere, six items that you would most enjoy, and the order in which these items mattered to you.

From a simple question, you conjured up all of that, without ever having to leave your chair.

How did you do this?

By retrieving, from your memory bank, every summer afternoon you've ever experienced, and mentally reengineering these memories into an afternoon that's absolutely perfect.

Because that's how Imagineering works.

Imagineering Is a Natural Brain Process

Imagineering is not something magical or mysterious—it's something our brains are naturally programmed to do.

We just saw how it operates in our 'perfect summer afternoon' exercise.

When confronted with a *What if?* question, our brain retrieves memories from its database—imprinted observations from the immediate, intermediate, or distant past.

Next, it sifts through, examines, organizes and selects situations, places, information, people and things that seem related to the question at hand.

Then it reengineers this data into something entirely new.

The brain engages in this reengineering activity because, like any computer, it follows the instruction it has been given.

In this case the command is: *What if?*

Imagineering is Reengineering Observations Stored in Your Mind

Accomplished creators have described the process by which we mentally engineer our observations and memories in various ways, using words like combining, blending, compounding, transposing, augmenting, mixing, imaging, and projecting.

Frank Wilczek, who won the Nobel Prize in Physics, has called it "systematic wishful thinking."

> *What is imagination, but the ability to consider what is not, but might be? Trying to make a scientific breakthrough, write a novel or compose a symphony, or create some other great work can be hard, frustrating work. Success is not guaranteed.*

Wishful thinking is an essential part of problem solving. It's very plausible, then, that an important step toward achievement, whether for machines or human beings, is to cultivate systematic wishful thinking.

Nickola Tesla, the engineer who invented the world's first alternating current (AC) motor, labeled it "improving and reconstructing."

When I get an idea, I start at once building it up in my imagination. I change the construction, make improvements, and operate the device in my mind. It is absolutely immaterial to me whether I run my turbine in my thought or test it in my shop. I even note if it is out of balance.

Steve Jobs said this mental reengineering is simply "connecting the dots" between what already exists, and what does not.

When you ask creative people how they did something, they feel a little guilty because they didn't really do it, they just saw something. It seemed obvious to them after a while.

That's because they were able to connect experiences they've had and synthesize new things. And the reason they were able to do that was that they've had more experiences or have thought more about their experiences than other people.

However you characterize it, the process is the same.

Our brain automatically pulls up what we have already observed in real life, and then reengineers it, providing us with an imaginary scenario, or mental blueprint, with which we can create something new.

Take a quick look back at some of the reinventions we've encountered so far in this book:

- Walt Disney reengineered 'Oswald the Lucky Rabbit' into Mickey Mouse.
- Eileen Fisher reengineered the kimono into stylish American clothes.
- Ted Turner reengineered satellite transmissions into CNN.
- Bob Dylan reengineered old songs into brand new hits.
- George de Mestral reengineered burs on his pants into Velcro.
- Mayo Clinic doctors reengineered cancer scans into pinpoint microscopes.

They all began the process by *observing* what already existed.

And then they asked themselves: *What if?*

When You Wish Upon a Star

While imagineering is something that naturally occurs, what distinguishes prolific creators from most everyone else is the central role that it plays in their lives.

Their brain's default mode is: *What If?*

Stephen Spielberg, the Oscar-winning producer and director, once described the way he reengineered his childhood memories in order to invent the main character in the wondrous and highly profitable movie, *E.T. The Extra Terrestrial*.

Notice the *What If's* in Spielberg's account.

> E.T. was never meant to be a movie about an extraterrestrial. It was meant to be a story about my mom and dad getting a divorce. I started writing a story about what it was like when your parents divide the family up, and they move to different states.
>
> I was working on (the E.T. script) before I made Close Encounters of the Third Kind. And when we filmed the scene in Close Encounters when the little alien, Puck, emerges from the mothership, it all came together in my mind. I thought, wait a second!
>
> What if that alien doesn't go back up into the ship?
>
> What if he stayed behind? Or what if he even got lost, and he was marooned here?
>
> What would happen if a child of a divorce, or a family of a divorce, with a huge hole to fill, filled the hole with his new best extraterrestrial friend?

Imagineering Tips from the Frankenstein Monster

Spielberg is hardly the only creator to reengineer personal observations into megahits.

Mary Shelley created the most popular monster story of all time, Frankenstein, by reengineering a nightmare that terrified her during a lightning-filled night on the shores of Lake Geneva, Switzerland.

She later recounted how it happened:

> *When I placed my head on my pillow I did not sleep, nor could I be said to think. My imagination, unbidden, possessed and guided me, gifting the successive images that arose in my mind with a vividness far beyond the usual bounds of reverie.*
>
> *I saw – with shut eyes, but acute mental vision – the pale student of the unhallowed arts kneeling beside the thing he had put together.*
>
> *I saw the hideous phantasm of a man stretched out, and then, on the working of some powerful engine, show signs of life and stir with an uneasy, half-vital motion.*
>
> *I opened my eyes in terror, as cheering was the idea that broke upon me: What terrified me will terrify others; and I need only describe the specter which had haunted my midnight pillow.*
>
> *On the morrow I announced that I had thought of a story. I began that day with the words, 'It was on a dreary night of November', making only a transcript of the grim terrors of my waking dream.*

Was Shelley asleep or awake when her mind invented Frankenstein?

Or was she somewhere in between?

To the average person, dreaming, or daydreaming, might seem like a strange strategy for creatively brainstorming breakthrough ideas, products or inventions.

But in reality, it's extremely powerful.

And, if our goal is to be creative in crucial situations, we'd be mistaken to dismiss it as anything less.

Throughout history, creative achievers have blueprinted some of their best, and most lucrative work, while asleep, half asleep, on a break, or otherwise zoned out.

And though it may have appeared to others that they were 'doing nothing much,' in actuality they were leveraging a purposeful strategy to tap into the power of their imaginations and their minds.

How can we personally benefit from their approach?

Here are some potent techniques to consider:

Technique #1
Think of Dreams and Daydreams as Imagineering Machines

During the mental haze between sleep and wakefulness, Paul McCartney ran to the piano to work out the first few chords of *Yesterday*, voted the #1 pop song of all time by *MTV* and *Rolling Stone* magazine.

> *I woke up one morning with a tune in my head, and I thought, 'Hey, I don't know this tune, or do I?' It was like a jazz melody. I went to the piano and found the chords to it, made sure I remembered it and then hawked it round to all my friends, asking what it was: 'Do you know this? It's a good little tune, but I couldn't have written it, because I dreamt it.'*

Salvador Dali, the famously eccentric Surrealist artist, characterized many of his most popular works as "hand painted dream photographs."

In his book for aspiring artists, *50 Secrets of Master Craftmanship*, he advised aspiring creators to do whatever's necessary to exploit the images their brains conjure up in semiconscious states.

He went so far as to recommend one of his favorite methods, which he called "slumber with a key."

This is Secret Number 3: You must resolve the problem of sleeping without sleeping, which separates sleeping from waking.

You must hold a heavy key, which you will keep suspended, delicately pressed between the extremities of the thumb and forefinger of your left hand. Having made these preparations, you will merely have to let yourself be progressively invaded by a serene afternoon nap.

Then, in the moment the key drops from your fingers, you may be sure that the noise of its fall will awaken you. For it is exactly, and neither more or less, what you needed before undertaking your afternoon labors.

Dali may have been half-kidding when he recommended this technique in 1949, but it turns out that he was way of ahead of his time, as neuroscientists have since discovered.

Technique #2
Don't Just Zone Out, Write It Down

Not long ago, among brain scientists, there was scant interest in dreaming, daydreaming or other forms of zoning out as keys to creative thinking.

That's since changed—a lot.

One of things they've discovered, through the use of state-of-the-art imaging technology, is that a human brain that's not engaged in conscious tasks naturally slips into what's called DMN—

default mode network — which allows it to sift through its inner database with unusual freedom and ease.

"Letting your mind drift off is the easy part," says Jonathan Schooler, a pioneer in the study of insight psychology at the University of California. "The hard part is maintaining enough awareness so that you can interrupt yourself and notice a creative thought."

"And that kind of awareness is the essence of creativity," according to Schooler.

Thus, the important thing to remember is this:

> **Before your insights fade from memory, be sure to write them down!**

Psychologist Eric Maisel calls this "productive concentration during an imaginative trance," adding that:

> *You need a quiet mind so that ideas will have a chance of connecting. You are hushing your mind so that you can use your mind. You are entrancing yourself. What do you see?*
>
> *Ideas will come to you as will images. Something that passes by in that hushed stillness may seem especially important. Give it a chance to grow more distinct. Hold it and nurture it until you can capture it.*

Technique #3
Take Your Trance for a Walk

Henry David Thoreau, one of America's first environmental thinkers and writers, wrote of his frequent wanderings through the woods of New England: "Methinks that the moment my legs begin to move, my thoughts begin to flow."

Indeed, history has shown, and modern psychology has explained, why creators often do some of their best work when they get up from their chairs and start wandering around.

There's even a technical name for this: *Think Walking*.

"Studies have shown that creative problems, in fact, can be solved by walking, particularly in nature, thanks to physiological changes in the brain that lead to lower frustration and stress," wrote Scott Kaufman and Carolyn Gregoire in their book *Wired to Create*.

Albert Einstein, who famously declared that "imagination is more important than knowledge," was perhaps the most productive wanderer of all.

Of the many reports about his eccentric behaviors in Princeton, New Jersey, where he lived and taught at the Institute for Advanced Study, perhaps the most instructive is included in Walter Isaacson's biography, *Albert Einstein: His Life and Universe*.

> *On his walk back home at midday, Einstein would often be joined by three or four professors or students. He would usually walk calmly and quietly, as if in a reverie, while they pranced around him, waved their arms, and tried to make their points.*
>
> *When they got to his house, the others would peel off, but Einstein sometimes just stood there thinking. His assistant, always watching from her window, would come outside, take his arm, and lead him inside for his macaroni lunch.*

So the next time it seems like the business or career challenges you face are as complex as the theory of relativity, why not give Einstein's method a try?

Invite your imagination out for a walk.

CHAPTER SEVEN

Actualization

Why Love Crafts the Final Result

S teve Jobs was wearing jeans and sandals under a black graduation gown as he stepped to the podium to deliver Stanford University's commencement address in 2005.

It was quite a scene, with some 23-thousand faculty members, alumni, newly-minted graduates and their parents jamming the field and bleachers of the school's football stadium, under nearly perfect Silicon Valley skies.

After all, who better than this icon of personal technology, the legendary entrepreneur who started Apple Computer - soon to be the world's most valuable company—to tell them how to capitalize on their knowledge-rich backgrounds?

The year before, the university's commencement speaker had been Supreme Court Justice Sandra Day O'Connor, and the year before that, Alejandro Toledo, the president of Peru.

Both held advanced degrees from Stanford and had admonished new graduates to pursue sober, serious careers.

So this year audience members must have been shocked out of their seats, when Jobs recommended a radically different approach to success:

> *You've got to find what you love. Your work is going to fill a large part of your life, and the only way to be truly satisfied is to do what you believe is great work. And the only way to do great work is to love what you do.*
>
> *If you haven't found it yet, keep looking. As with all matters of the heart, you'll know when you find it. And, like any great relationship, it just gets better and better as the years roll on. So keep looking until you find it – don't settle.*
>
> *This approach has never let me down, and it has made all the difference in my life.*

Perhaps the biggest difference came in 1985, a decade after Jobs and electronic engineer Steve Wozniak started Apple in Job's parent's garage, and began building it into a $2-billion-dollar company.

Soon after releasing Apple's first revolutionary Macintosh computer, Jobs had an ugly falling out with then-CEO John Sculley, who subsequently arranged to have Jobs fired.

It was a triple whammy – a personal, career and business crisis like nothing Jobs could have imagined.

> *What had been the focus of my entire adult life was gone, and it was devastating. I really didn't know what to do for a few months. I was a very public failure, and I even thought about running away from Silicon Valley.*

ACTUALIZATION

But something slowly began to dawn on me — I still loved what I did. The turn of events at Apple had not changed that one bit. I had been rejected, but I was still in love. And so I decided to start over.

I didn't see it then, but it turned out that getting fired from Apple was the best thing that could have ever happened to me. The heaviness of being successful was replaced by the lightness of being a beginner again, less sure about everything.

It freed me to enter one of the most creative periods of my life. During the next five years, I started a company named NeXT, and bought another company named Pixar, which is now the most successful animation studio in the world.

Sometimes life hits you in the head with a brick. Don't lose faith. I'm convinced that the only thing that kept me going was that I loved what I did.

In this chapter and the next, we'll examine how skills and abilities that we love to use — including those we may have relished using early in life and since forgotten about — can propel us to unanticipated levels of creativity when a business or career crisis strikes.

> **Actualization is the third act in the practice of crucial creativity.**
> It is by leveraging skills and abilities that they love to use that creative achievers transform what they've imagined into reality.

What skills and abilities have *you* personally loved using over the course of your life?

How might you potentially leverage these to reinvent your business or career?

Later, we'll hone in on these questions in some depth as you develop a personalized inventory of skills to chronicle your answers.

But first, let's see why love is so crucial in creating your future success.

From Litigation to Funny Business

For many of us, the business or career path that we're on, even if sufficient for financial survival or comfort, may offer us little in the way of personal joy, meaning, or satisfaction.

We anxiously wonder: is this really all there is to life? We intuitively sense that there may be solutions to our professional doldrums, but we're unsure how to discover them.

Sometimes it takes a crisis to find out.

That's exactly what happened to Harvard Law School graduate Justin Shanes, who, after three years at one of New York's top legal firms, couldn't wait to pull the plug on his prestigious position as a young corporate litigator.

"My three year stint in law was, to put it mildly, soul withering," said Justin. "I hated the emphasis on billable hours. I hated being called into the office on a Sunday because a partner felt like escaping his family."

To temper his misery, Justin began taking improvisation classes and writing comedy sketches in his off hours "basically seizing on every excuse for creativity I could. Those joyous moments kept me sane on days when I wanted to lower my head into the paper shredder tongue first."

As a youngster, Justin had somehow always felt connected to funny business.

"At summer camp, I passed up softball to read MAD magazine and take electives like 'Television and Puppetry,' he recalled. My high school friends and I spent our Saturday nights shooting talk show parodies in my parents' basement."

But make a career of such silliness?

The very idea seemed detached from reality, growing up in a neighborhood like his, "where bragging about your child's career was a competitive sport."

As his unhappiness grew in his law career, he began observing and meeting other New Yorkers who were earnestly trying to turn comedy into their livelihood.

Hanging out with these fellow aspiring 'creative types,' seeing them seriously make a go of it, generated a shift in his outlook — from "not a shot," to "why not at least give it a try?"

Finally, Justin gave notice at the offices of Hogan & Hartson, and made what he called a "glamorous comedic debut" performing a standup bit in the basement of a neighborhood Mexican restaurant, before an audience, as he put it, of "exactly five."

His trajectory from there was hardly a straight line.

But long story short: he refused to give up.

After multiple successive, if undistinguished on-stage appearances, friends in the comedy field managed to help Justin land a job as a writer on NBC's *Late Night with Jimmy Fallon* show, at a salary roughly equivalent to what he'd earned as an attorney.

Explained Justin: "Everybody wanted to know if I felt vindicated about leaving the law. In a certain sense, sure. Obviously tangible success is not irrelevant. But the real vindication came well before *Fallon*."

It came, said Justin, during those first few minutes "competing with the nearby fajita sizzle" downstairs at the Mexican bistro.

"For me, recapturing a sense of purpose was the win. It didn't matter how big the crowd or prestigious the venue. That I could get up on stage and confidently deliver some remarkably stupid jokes made it all worthwhile. There would be no more what-ifs, no regrets as an old man looking back on his life."

It took a crisis of meaning for Justin to painstakingly transform his first love — being funny — into his actual business.

Doing What You Love Can Save You

While some vocational crises, like Justin Shane's, may strike early in life, others may impact us further down the career track.

Either way, our love for using particular skills and abilities can play a vital role in our reinvention.

Marion Rosen is a perfect case in point.

Trained in both psychology and physical therapy, Marion built a successful practice in the San Francisco area, treating people with pain and injuries through a uniquely personal method she'd developed by blending psychotherapy with bodywork techniques.

For decades, she enjoyed a reliable stream of patient referrals from physicians in nearby clinics and hospitals — until the financial crisis she'd long worried about came to pass: many of the doctors she knew began to retire.

As a result, her patient base dried up.

Nearing age 60, with no pension or other income, Marion faced what looked like a bleak, forced retirement of her own.

Her expectations, she told me, were that she would "just wait it out until I got Social Security and sit down and wait until I died. That's what I thought would happen."

Fortunately, she was way off.

Instead, the daughter of a former patient phoned Marion with an invitation: would she be willing to teach her, and a group of friends, Marion's personal method, so that they might open 'Rosen Method' practices of their own?

At first Marion was reluctant, worried that her inherent shyness, and lack of teaching experience, might prove humiliating and cause her to fail.

But after mustering enough courage to lead a few initial workshops, she found herself falling in love with the process of teaching and coaching others.

The experience, Marion later explained, dramatically shifted her perspective:

> *Whatever happens to you, there are possibilities there. Maybe we just don't see them at first. Like in my case you can say no, I can't do that. Or you can say, well, I haven't tried. I haven't done that before.*
>
> *We should just respond to whatever shows up, because you can never tell what will show up next.*

What showed up in Marion's programs, over the next several years, were hundreds of psychologists, physical therapists, and professional dancers, all wanting to personally benefit from, and learn how to share her techniques with others.

Over time, Marion and this growing cadre of instructors established training centers in the United States, and nearly every corner of the world.

Marion's unexpected love for skills she never previously knew she had, not only saved her from a meager and depressing retirement, but helped launch new careers and businesses for a global community of Rosen Method practitioners that continues to flourish today.

Love Is the Common Denominator

Let's quickly recap some of what we've seen in this chapter so far:

- Steve Jobs' love for his design and marketing work sustained him through the dark days after being fired from Apple, and empowered him to enter one of the most creative periods of his life.

- Justin Shane's lifelong love for comedy writing and performance unshackled him from the law career that he despised, and opened the way for a new line of work that fulfilled his dreams and aspirations.

- Marion Rosen's love for teaching, newly discovered in her 60's, became the foundation for a business and career reinvention beyond anything she ever imagined, as well as the launch pad for an international enterprise.

When you flip back to the words, and stories, of other creative achievers we've met in this book, you often see the same phenomenon at work:

- Walt Disney fell in love with drawing when he was six years old, and was unceasingly passionate about his cartooning skills for the rest of his life.

- Eileen Fisher was so smitten with the idea of designing simple, modular women's wear, she built a global enterprise around the concept.
- Albert Einstein was so fascinated with the inner workings of the universe, he often stood mesmerized while developing equations in his mind.

Pioneering psychologist Mihaly Csikszentmihalyi, who originated the concept of 'being in flow,' or 'in the zone,' explained the link between love and creative achievement like this:

> *Creative persons differ from one another in a variety of ways, but in one respect they are unanimous: they all love what they do. The excitement of the artist at the easel or the scientist in the lab comes close to the ideal fulfillment we all hope to get from life, but rarely do.*

Based on his research, concluded Csikszentmihalyi, the message that highly creative people are sending is: career success and personal fulfillment are the natural outgrowths of applying the skills and abilities—doing the kind of work—that you love.

Why the Skills You Love Supercharge Your Creativity

Still, you may wonder: how much difference can using skills and abilities that you love really make when you're in the grips of a crisis? When you're trying to reinvent your business or career on a trajectory that's rocky and unclear?

The short answer: all the difference in the world.

There's a long history to the quote "Creativity is 1% inspiration and 98% perspiration," various versions of which have been attributed to Thomas Edison and others.

Whoever said this first, and however exactly they put it, the point is inarguable and clear.

While creativity can be exhilarating, there are frequently times, particularly during the Actualization phase of crucial creativity, when even the most motivated person can lose faith.

Why?

Because Actualization—the act of transforming what we've imagined into material form—is a uniquely demanding task.

Jordan Roth, the Tony Award-winning Broadway producer, explains:

> *You have an idea that you're unpacking and exploring and grappling with and trying to express. And how you express it, and the craftsmanship of that expression, is the difference between good and great.*
>
> *Or may even be the difference between great and life-changing.*

The perspiration necessary to meet this challenge, the uncertainty of the outcome—these are the reasons why it's critically important to love the work that we're doing, to relish the skills and abilities that we bring to bear in actualizing our reinventive plans.

We can't create on an empty tank of commitment.

We need refills of energy to keep going, to manage and overcome the false starts, setbacks, recalibrations and occasional full stops that will inevitably come our way.

It might be useful to think of every career or business reinvention like one of those home renovation shows on TV:

Once the blueprints are complete, and the homeowners are excited about the project, the work gets underway. Then inevitably, a few days or weeks in, the contractor advises them that the kitchen wiring he located is so faulty, and the bathroom plumbing is leaking so badly, it will all need to be replaced.

Applying the lessons of this example to all reinventive undertakings: we must always be prepared to delete the first business strategy we've devised, dump the half-finished career plans, or delay the new product rollout we've scheduled, until all the kinks can be fully worked out.

When this happens, as it inevitably will, we *will need the love of our skills and abilities*, of our craft, to take us, and our creative venture, through the obstacle course, and over the next hill.

The Joy and Power of Flow

Steve Jobs wasn't just offering his personal opinion in 2005 when he told young, graduating Stanford students: "the only way to do great work is to love what you do."

Behind this statement are decades of research into human performance and success that apply to people in every creative field and endeavor.

Listen for a moment as National Book Award-winning author, and respected surgeon, Sherwin B. Nuland, describes his experience of writing:

> *It gives me an extraordinary feeling. You really detach from anything else. You have the sense that something is coming out of you. It is a physical sense. It's an emotional sense. The outside world is lost to you.*
>
> *When you're enjoying something as intensely as that, you feel that you're physically, not just emotionally, but physically part of it. It's a sense that you are doing something beautiful and therefore you're beautiful. The writing just flows along, page after page after page.*

Dr. Nuland's sense of detachment and experience of beauty are among the well-documented elements of the *flow experience*, a scientifically quantifiable condition in which our attention and skills are so fully engaged that our performance is enhanced well beyond our usual levels of achievement.

What is it that triggers this unique state of being?

> *Using skills and abilities that we love, to meet a challenge that personally inspires us.*

Peak performance expert Mihaly Csikszentmihalyi found overwhelming evidence for this in his dozens of interviews with a broad spectrum of highly creative people.

> *We found the same sentiments in every single interview.*

What is extraordinary is that we talked to engineers and chemists, writers and musicians, businesspersons and social reformers, historians and architects, sociologists and physicians — and they all agree that they do what they do primarily because it's fun.

We also need a positive goal, otherwise why keep going?

As Csikszentmihalyi documented, and creative achievers in every field have testified: when you love what you do, and face off against challenges that inspire you, the results that you produce will, quite naturally, be your best possible work.

Coming up next............

In the next chapter, we'll examine a phenomenon that's uncommonly reported on: the sudden emergence of skills and abilities that we never knew we possessed.

And we'll begin to compile a *Personalized Inventory of Skills & Abilities* for you to work with, as you start framing up your own business or career reinvention.

CHAPTER EIGHT

How Crucial Skills Appear

Crisscrossing the U.S. while doing research for this book, one of the places I found myself was deep inside a North Carolina pine forest, where giant metal flowers appeared to be growing out of the ground.

Had these lovely figures been planted there, or taken root on their own in the moist soil?

The stems were so life-like, and the petals so vibrantly colored, that my experience of walking among them was simultaneously natural and surreal.

It's often said that powerful art evokes in us surprising emotions and sensations.

And in a way I couldn't grasp at the time, I felt comforted — it somehow seemed as though the metal flowers and their surroundings belonged together, that their intermingling made natural sense.

Several weeks later, 25-hundred miles west of that forest, I had an entirely different feeling.

Standing in the lobby of a Los Angeles office building, I sensed a bolt of energy surging through me as I gaped at large, high contrast photographs of Cuban dancers swirling through the streets in Havana; of American construction workers pirouetting on girders hundreds of feet in the air; of Parisian bicyclists kissing as they crossed the Seine.

Far more unexpected, even, than my experiences of these highly distinct creations — the calming metal flowers and the powerful photographs — was this astonishing fact:

These impactful works had been created by individuals who, before facing significant personal and career crises, had never produced anything like them, or considered themselves capable of doing so.

In the process of reinvention, they discovered crucial skills and abilities they never knew they had.

How did this happen?

Is it possible that we all harbor, within us, hidden skills and abilities?

Is a particular mindset, or perspective, required to uncover and put these capabilities to work?

In this chapter, we'll see how Rita Spina, a career clinical psychologist, unpredictably became a much-in-demand environmental artist, known for creating, among other works, the remarkable metal flowers I encountered.

And we'll visit with Gil Garcetti who, after being fired from one of America's highest profile legal positions, suddenly began producing powerful photographs that would grace the walls of businesses, galleries and museums nationwide.

Through their stories, we'll see how previously undiscovered skills and abilities empowered them to reinvent their livelihoods, and we'll learn the neuroscientific secrets behind this.

Rita K. Spina
Rediscovering Long Forgotten Skills

Observation

In her mid-60's, Rita Spina received an emergency phone call, informing her that her twenty five years of marriage had come to a tragic end: her husband had died from a heart attack while playing tennis with friends.

His passing, Rita told me, left her totally on her own:

> *And I went through a really tough time because he had set the foundation, you know, between the two of us, the foundation that we were going to live on. After he was gone, there was no guideline for me – he wasn't coming home.*

Rita's personal crisis coincided with a career breakdown that had been brewing for some time: after more than four decades as a clinical psychologist, she no longer enjoyed the work she once loved – she was burned out.

> *What I really needed was to turn away from it. I closed my old psychology books and stuck them in a big box in the attic, and that was the end of it.*
>
> *I still wanted to accomplish something, to continue developing myself. That's the way I'd always been. But I had no idea where I was going, no thoughts in my mind.*

Where Rita did go was out to Oregon to visit with her daughter, who was living in Portland at the time.

Hoping to relax one sunny morning, on a leisurely drive from Portland to the Oregon Coast, Rita found herself surrounded by huge logging trucks on the highway, and outraged by the payload they carried.

Years later, recalling the experience, her voice still trembled.

> *The loggers had cut down all the historic old growth forests, and in the most beautiful spaces there was nothing left but stubs. And I was just struck by it, and actually felt nauseous about it.*
>
> *Our heritage, as a country, was forever lost. And when I came back home to North Carolina where I lived, I just couldn't forget it.*

Over time, her emotions evolved: she began to experience a sense that there was something she needed to do about what she'd observed.

What skills or opportunities did she, as a psychologist, have to express her feelings—and who would pay attention?

Perhaps something—an epiphany or realization of some kind would come to her?

Then again, maybe not.

Imagineering

Back home, she developed a new habit of taking long and seemingly-aimless walks through the southern pine forests behind her house.

And for reasons that were unclear, as yet, she found herself collecting natural debris, particularly fallen branches with interesting shapes, which she stored in her garage.

She wondered what was happening to her. Why was she gathering this stuff? Was she suddenly becoming a hoarder?

She had no clue.

But you and I, having explored the way imagineering works (Chapter 6) might have explained what Rita later came to understand: she was *think walking*, like Albert Einstein, as her brain unconsciously began engineering mental blueprints of ways in which she might convert her feelings into some form of material expression.

As she explained:

> *Walking in the forest, I would collect old pieces of wood and stuff like that, and it felt somehow or another like it was all related, focused around what I had seen and experienced in Oregon.*
>
> *At around the same time, I began going to junkyards and finding materials that were natural, different types of wood and other materials that were part of the organic aspects of the world. I also picked up discarded things that had been man made, things that reflected change and technological progress.*
>
> *Back in my garage, I began to put these elements together in three-dimensional pieces that you might very roughly call artwork.*
>
> *And I began to get ideas about how these two things – wood and man-made material – played off of one another. I found, for example, that if you turn an old, discarded golf club upside down, you can transform it into an iron flower.*

> *And I thought: 'which was going to win? Was it the world and its natural self, or the manufactured world, the world of progress and development? Or was it possible for them to somehow work, live together, side by side?'*
>
> *And this became the concept, the message I somehow wanted to send, if I could figure out how.*

Actualization

Rita had always been an art lover—as a girl, she'd poured over art books and attended classes at the Parson's School of Design in New York City, where she grew up.

But she'd never seriously considered art as a career path. Instead, she put her creative passions aside to earn a PhD in clinical psychology, which she later practiced in school, corporate and private settings.

It took the shock of the Oregon clear cutting experience to reawaken the long-suppressed artist inside her.

> *As a kid, what had been stored in my psyche somehow was that some day when I had time, I would again start to explore that piece of myself, which was the world of art. And here I was finally doing that!*
>
> *As a psychologist, I'd always put people and ideas together. Now, I was putting things and ideas together. But would my art be any good? Would the message ever get out there? That, I didn't know.*

As her imagination conjured up potential art forms, artistic skills that she'd loved learning in high school—like design and brush painting—seemed to come back to her quickly.

At the same time, she began learning new skills, such as sculpting and welding, which sparked her interest and attention.

Perhaps as importantly, she started to discover that the community where she lived was filled with creators, some of them accomplished artists who took her under their wings, helped her to hone her abilities, and eventually persuaded her to display her work at a local art exhibition and sale.

That's where everything changed.

> *It was a situation where the seven other people in the exhibition had been artists for years and years. Here I was, a brand new person. And somebody bought my first piece. I was totally shocked.*
>
> *Now, all of a sudden I felt like I was a genuine artist. And it was at that point it became a new career for me.*
>
> *Even now, years later, I'm not always confident. But I know when something I'm creating is good and I know when it's not. I've learned to take something I'm doing and look at it more critically and, if I need to, tear it up and throw it out. Or, I can just put it away until another time, when I'll pull it out and go back at it again.*

Rita never returned to practicing psychology. Instead, she set up a small studio in her home, which also served as a gallery where visitors could view, and purchase, her creations.

Over the next several years, her work started to be featured in exhibitions, studio tours and competitive art shows throughout North Carolina, where she gained a reputation as an artist with a message — that nature and mankind *can* beautifully coexist, if only we make a conscious effort to bring them together.

What Explains This?

As Rita indicated in our conversations, she was astounded that, after years of viewing herself solely as a psychologist, she had suddenly begun creating artwork that people wanted to own.

"I didn't think anybody would want it, so it was amazing to me that somebody bought it, because I had just figured that I would take it home with me after the show was over."

Undoubtedly the biggest shock was not that she could envision the artwork before she made it — as a psychologist she understood how imagineering works — but that she could find within herself, or learn to develop, the professional-level artistic skills necessary to craft what she'd imagined into material form.

Turns out, she needn't have been surprised — and neither should you or I.

Why? Because, in recent years, state-of-the-art brain science has turned on its head practically everything we once believed about acquiring and developing skills.

Consider the expression "you can't teach an old dog new tricks," which ranks among the oldest proverbs in the English language.

It's so commonly used that it appears in nearly every major dictionary. The respected Cambridge Dictionary, for example, explains its meaning like this: "it is very difficult to teach someone new skills or to change someone's habits or characters."

But no matter how many times we repeat, or have been led to believe this, it's totally untrue.

At the turn of the 21st Century, pioneering neuroscientist Michael Merzenich, based at the University of California, was the first to provide scientific evidence of this to his colleagues and the world.

He called his discovery *neuroplasticity*.

The Neuroscience of Creative Potential

Through his revolutionary experiments with 'brain mapping' in animals, and later humans, Merzenich demonstrated that our brain, previously believed to grow rigid and inflexible after childhood, is, in actuality, able to continuously remodel, rewire and improve itself *if* – and this is the key – we continue to teach it new tricks.

If, like budding artist Rita Spina, we make the effort to put latent, perhaps long-forgotten skills to work, while continuing to learn and develop new ones.

When I met with Dr. Merzenich, I asked him to elaborate.

> **Mark**: *One of the things I've seen in some of the people I've studied are leaps in abilities – that is, they seem to quickly develop hidden skills or abilities in areas you would never expect. So for instance, a psychologist who became a successful artist, or an attorney who became a brilliant photographer.*
>
> *Is it your sense that we all have hidden skills and capabilities?*
>
> **Dr. Merzenich**: *Of course we do, and we also always have within us the ability to step life up a notch in whatever we're doing, to carry ourselves to a higher level of operations or extend our operations.*
>
> *The brain, in fact, is continuously changing, Mark. It's continuously changing and revising its wiring, as a consequence of what you do. And each time you acquire a new skill or ability or take on a new set of challenges that requires new learning on a substantial level, the brain is remodeling itself.*

We're continuously plastic. We have the capacity to change to the end of our life. We have the capacity to be stronger and better, to have deeper understanding, to improve our capacities, to extend our abilities at any point of life.

Gil Garcetti
Finding Skills Hidden in Plain Sight

In discussing career reinventions with Dr. Merzenich, the other person I mentioned to him, besides Rita, was a high profile attorney who uncovered previously-hidden skills as remarkable as hers, when he was suddenly struck by a career crisis of his own.

If the name Gil Garcetti rings a bell, it's likely because Gil was the nationally-known Los Angeles District Attorney whose office prosecuted the notorious O.J. Simpson murder trial.

Several years after Simpson was acquitted, voters threw Gil out of his job.

As a career civil servant, he'd never earned much money, he told me, and had no idea what path to pursue.

The day after my election loss, I'm emotionally bruised, angry, and upset. I didn't only want to be able to contribute to my family, I also wanted to make a difference in the world. Even if it was just a small tiny, tiny, tiny bit.

While he didn't have a clear career plan, he did have a hobby, maybe even a bit of an obsession, to hear him tell it.

I had started carrying a camera with me wherever I went right after my daughter was born. And I got in the habit of always having it with me, because you never know what you're going to see.

> *For example, I was walking to the office one day and just before I got to the criminal courts building I heard this boom. And I looked over and saw that a car had run into a transit bus, right under the sign where it said 'welcome aboard.' What a sight! And so I took some photos of it.*
>
> *Why? I just loved taking photographs. I found a satisfaction and a personal reward in it. I wasn't doing it for any other reason.*
>
> *I'd never had any training, although I did start going to a high school adult night class in photography at one point. But I wasn't thinking that I was going to become a professional photographer at any time.*
>
> *It was a hobby – an intense hobby.*

What Gil didn't fully recognize was how fine a photographer all this ad hoc practice had made him. Or how the skills that he'd developed as a prosecutor—his ability to rapidly assess and absorb details at any scene or location—had given him an advantage that other photographers might never have.

> *As a prosecutor, I was always seeing things that other people would look at but didn't see. And I'd say, 'well didn't you see that? You were looking right at it!'*
>
> *I'm not saying that I'm any better than them, but I saw something there that was of interest. It could be the design, the geometry of it, whatever was intriguing to me. I wanted to capture that for myself, but I also wanted to share it with others.*

Six months after leaving the D.A.'s office, everything seemed to come together for Gil in a moment of perfect synchronicity—he found himself, with his camera, in the right place at precisely the right time.

> *It was a happenstance encounter. I'm at a meeting downtown. A volunteer board that I'm on, and I'm leaving, starting to drive home.*
>
> *I'm between the Dorothy Chandler Pavilion and the then-being-built Walt Disney Concert Hall. And I look up and see this one iron worker who is literally on all fours, crawling over a high arch beam way, way up in the sky. And I thought: 'Whoa, wait a minute, I have to photograph this guy!'*
>
> *So I took a few snapshots, and then came back the next morning with bigger camera equipment. And from across the street I saw this guy again, way up in the air. To him, he was just doing his job. To me he was like a dare devil.*
>
> *I realized: 'this is marvelous! Look at the beauty of this geometry of the iron, the raw steel that's there. But I'm way across the street, how do I get on site?' So I made a phone call and eventually made the connection with some of my union friends, and they let me onto the construction site.*

Over a period of several months, Gil kept returning to the construction site and, at their request, started giving copies of the photos he was taking to the "daredevil" workers who were his subjects.

They were flattered and flabbergasted — to their eyes, Gil's photos were truly excellent. So much so, that they kept insisting that he compile and publish his work in a book.

They promised him that the structure they were constructing was destined to become a world-famous building — and that everyone was going to remember Frank Gehry, the architect who designed it, but nobody was going to remember them.

At first, Gil vehemently resisted, afraid that anyone outside of the tight-knit construction team who viewed his photos would see them for what they were: the work of an amateur, a neophyte, who didn't know what he was doing.

But the workers kept nudging him on.

> *I finally said, 'okay, I'll do it.' My fear was that some publisher would take my notoriety as the former District Attorney and publish the photographs for a quick buck and then I'd get panned. And that would be the end of my photographic career, if I ever was going to have one, for sure.*
>
> *But as it turned out, I was convinced by people at the Los Angeles philharmonic, whose home would be the new Disney concert hall, as well as several respected critics, that the photographs would stand on their own. Forget me or who I was. So that's how my first book: Iron: Erecting the Walt Disney Concert Hall came out.*
>
> *Not long after, I knew things in my life had really changed when two things happened almost immediately. One was that the Los Angeles Times, which was my nemesis when I was the D.A., all of a sudden couldn't say enough good things about me as a photographer. They were praising me to the hilt.*
>
> *The other was that, out of the blue, a major law firm contacts me, because they bought the book, saying they want to buy ten or twelve photographs. And I'm walking to the office carrying the photographs when I literally stopped and said, 'wait a minute, this law firm is not a law firm full of my friends!'*

> *The person who contacted me I didn't know from Adam. They wouldn't be paying the kind of money they were paying for these photographs unless they thought they were really worth it, because law firms are notoriously cheap.*
>
> *And I said, 'they must be pretty good'. So that was a reaffirmation to me that maybe I do have something here with my photography.*

Three years, and numerous other photo projects, books, and public exhibitions later, Gil earned the right to be totally confident of this, when the prestigious *American Photo Magazine* named him one of the country's four master photographers.

What's the X-Factor Behind This?

When all is said and done, is there some secret, some unique element that drives dramatic, unexpected transformations like Gil's and Rita's?

A distinctive factor that might allow any of us to tap into previously unrecognized skills and abilities while inventing, or reinventing a business or career?

For the answer, I turned again to Dr. Michael Merzenich, the neuroscientist who literally mapped every inch, and assessed every chemical, running through the human brain.

> **Mark:** *What's the most important thing, or what are the most important things that we need to do in order to make these great leaps in our abilities? How do we think or program ourselves, or train ourselves, or exercise our minds?*

Dr. Merzenich: *You need to be working at something you care about — something you love. It has to matter to you. One of the ways to think about how you could define where you belong or how you could strengthen or elaborate yourself is you could say 'Well, what's important to me? What's exciting to me? What's rewarding to me? What makes me happy?'*

One of the really interesting things that we commonly see when people transform themselves is that they're not just doing something at a mundane level. We often see that they've found what they were really meant to do in life, and they take a great leap forward in the extension of their potential and possibility. They suddenly move into the domain that they were really constructed for.

Let's say you've always had a dream that you would really love to do something. If that's so, then it's worth pursuing, and that's the way to think about it. Because what that means is that when you get into the activity, if it is in fact continuously rewarding and positive, you will be changing your brain in ways that empower you.

Through decades of studying how the brain operates, Dr. Merzenich scientifically established, and quantified, what people like Rita Spina and Gil Garcetti learned from personal experience:

When we discover, or rediscover, skills and abilities that we love to use, we expand the boundaries of our creativity.

Discovering Your Creative Skills & Abilities

On the next several pages you will find two user-friendly tools:

- A sampling of skills and abilities that are commonly involved in creating successful business ventures and careers.

- A template designed to help you identify personal skills and abilities that you have loved using, and that may prove valuable to you in creating your future.

Working with these tools, you will start to compile a *Personal Inventory of Skills & Abilities* for use later in the book, as you begin to design a personal framework for business or career reinvention.

Sampling of Skills & Abilities for Crucial Creativity

This is not intended to be a complete list of every area in which you may have skills or abilities. Be sure to include others that you have used when you compile your Personal Inventory on the next page.

Business, Marketing, Advertising	Mathematics
Computers, Internet	Engineering
Law	Athletics, Recreation
Medicine	Auto, Motorcycle, Boating, Aircraft
Finance	Education, Training
Psychiatry, Psychology	Research and Development
Physical Therapy, Bodywork	Analysis, Diagnostics
Science	Building, Construction Work

Visual and Graphic Arts	Gardening, Horticulture
Music	Electrical Work, Electronics
Handicraft, Decorative Arts	Film, Video
Performing	Mechanics
Writing, Editing	Fashion, Clothing
Speaking, Storytelling	Woodworking, Metalworking
Photography	Design, Architecture
Computers	Environment

Organizing, Coordinating	Compromising, Listening
Persuading, Selling, Lobbying	Directing, Delegating
Negotiating, Mediating	Simplifying, Conceptualizing
Motivating	Promoting, Marketing
Explaining, Communicating	Role Playing
Teaching, Coaching, Advising	Coaching, Mentoring
Mentoring, Guiding	Sympathizing, Supporting
Facilitating Change	Inspiring

Personal Inventory of Skills & Abilities

Using the previous page as a reference point, begin to create an inventory of skills and abilities that you currently love using or have previously loved using in your life, education, business or career.

Jot down your inventory on this page or compile it elsewhere, and as you think of additional skills and abilities over time, be sure to add them to your list. Later in the book, we will use this inventory to begin 'framing up' your future.

Note: On the pages that follow, look over the schematics of Rita and Gil's strategies for reinvention that revolve around their newly-discovered creative skills. As you compile your personal inventory, keep in mind that you may have hidden skills too!

Rita K. Spina's Crucial Creativity

Crisis Faced: Career Burnout, Personal Tragedy

OBSERVE
Rita observed that chainsaw clear cutting of evergreen forests had ravaged the natural beauty of the legendary Oregon Trail.

IMAGINEER
Always an art lover, Rita began imagining new forms of artwork that would portray man and nature coexisting in beauty and harmony.

ACTUALIZE
Rita rediscovered long-forgotten artistic skills she had loved learning in high school, and merged them with new skills she developed, to make the original forms of artwork she had imagined real.

OUTCOME
A unique brand of artwork and a new career and business, marrying man-made and natural materials to portray peaceful coexistence between nature and mankind.

Gil Garcetti's Crucial Creativity

Crisis Faced: Voted out of office as L.A. District Attorney

OBSERVE
Gil observed that ironworkers constructing the Walt Disney concert hall looked like daredevil acrobats in the sky.

IMAGINEER
Gil envisioned powerful photographs showing the dangers of the ironworkers job, and the grace with which they performed it.

ACTUALIZE
Gil leveraged the photographic skills that he loved developing as a hobbyist and while a prosecutor, to capture the essence of a location or scene.

OUTCOME
Publication of a book of photographs entitled *Iron: Erecting the Walt Disney Concert Hall*, which launched Gil's new career and business as one of America's master photographers.

PART THREE

Never Waste a Crisis

CHAPTER NINE

Meeting the Moment

On March 25th of 2020, the night that New York City ordered its thousands of eateries to shut down in the face of the COVID-19 crisis, Gabrielle Hamilton, proprietor of the highly popular Prune restaurant in the East Village, enjoyed a last supper with her staff and wished them an indefinite farewell.

She looked everybody in the eye and said: "I've decided not to wait and see what will happen. I encourage you to call first thing in the morning for unemployment, and you have a week's paycheck coming from me."

Over the next month, as her city became one of the world's fastest-growing coronavirus hot spots, Gabrielle sat in her shuttered bistro and put her thoughts down on paper, writing:

> *I, like hundreds of other chefs across the city and thousands across the country, are now staring down the question of what our restaurants, our careers, our lives, might look like if we even get them back.*

> *I have been shuttered before. Prune has survived 9/11, the blackout, Hurricane Sandy, the recession, and months of a city water-main replacement.*

So I'm going to let the restaurant sleep, like the beauty she is, shallow breathing, dormant. And yet even with the gate indefinitely shut against the coronavirus, I've been dreaming again.

As we've seen throughout this book, we human beings are dreamers and creators.

By instinct or with strategic intent, we observe the way things are, ask ourselves *What If?*, and set about the work of constructing solutions, innovations and inventions to create a better future.

> **Observation > Imagineering > Actualization**

We employ this formula — these three acts of creativity — to improve our business or career when times are good, and we use it with a sense of crucial urgency when crisis strikes.

In just the first six months of the coronavirus crisis, numerous examples of our creative ingenuity were vividly on display — let's take a glance at a few.

> "No other area offers richer opportunities for successful innovation than the unexpected."
> *-Peter F. Drucker, Father of Modern Management*

From Playgrounds to Outdoor Classrooms

From the time he first observed TV images of emergency hospitals under construction in Wuhan, China, it became clear to Adam Bienenstock that his business might be headed for a crash.

For decades his company, Bienenstock Natural Playgrounds, had designed and manufactured outdoor wooden playground equipment for parks, schools and day care centers.

But prompted by early warnings from his father—a respected immunologist—Adam began to envision the day when COVID-19 could cross international borders and force children in North America to be sheltered at home.

Adam later recalled:

> *I was looking at the virus case numbers and seeing how fast they were growing in China, and I was directly translating that to our business.*
>
> *As soon as there's a lockdown, I figured, that means kids will stop going to school, and schools will stop purchasing what we manufacture. And if kids stop going to childcare, that means childcare centers will go bankrupt.*
>
> *So I was making these extrapolations pretty fast, like 'this is not good.'*
>
> *The only surprise was that it took until March for the pandemic to really hit, and by February we were well underway with our plans for turning things around.*

By mid-Spring of 2020, when schools were indeed shutting down, Adam's company had already reengineered its core product line, and had begun to manufacture a new offering that could help bring students safely back to class.

They called it *OutClass*—outdoor classrooms, featuring weather-resistant desks, blackboards and supply cabinets that could be set up in less than a day, and based on prevailing scientific evidence, provide a more virus-protective learning environment than rooms inside the walls of school buildings.

By early fall, Adam's company had already manufactured and delivered some 120 of these new outdoor learning setups to schools in the U.S. and Canada, and had received calls and emails about installing hundreds more.

"Outdoor environments have been shown to improve educational outcomes," he told me, "plus these new *OutClass* products can be converted into playground structures once the virus crisis subsides."

"This is more than a quick fix for our company — we view it as a long term play."

> "The pandemic has been a catalyst for shifting to the cloud"
> -Rajat Bhargava, Founder & CEO, JumpCloud

From Wine Cellars to Virtual Tastings

Faced with plunging sales as social distancing mandates took hold, John Kapon, chairman of Acker wines, a 200-year-old rare and fine wine firm, reinvented his business model, by moving his tasting room and auction gallery into cyberspace.

How exactly did this work?

John devised a system allowing wine aficionados to order select vintages online, prior to interactive tasting sessions on Zoom and Instagram Live, led personally by John and other respected wine experts.

During the first month of these new internet-based tasting programs, his direct consumer e-commerce sales shot up 300%.

John explained:

> *The backbone of our company is to drink and share great wines with our clients. Wine is meant to be shared. The Zoom format allows you to be with 50 or 60 people at a time.*

In normal times, in-person wine auctions in New York and Hong Kong were even more vital to John's business than consumer purchases, so he moved these online, as well.

As a result, his firm reaped $7-million through virtual bidding in the first quarter of 2020, enough to persuade him to continue these unique online programs even when in-person tastings and auctions resumed.

> "When things get bad enough, it forces people to come together and come up with ideas."
> -William C. Rudin, President, Rudin Real Estate Management

From One Kind of Real Estate to Another

Crises have often led to reinventions in commercial real estate and, as of mid-2020, the coronavirus crisis was expected to set new records.

With the pandemic accelerating the closure of retail stores, shopping malls and hotels nationwide, tens of millions of square feet of vacant or underutilized property were on track to be converted to new uses.

In New York, for example, Amazon announced its decision to transform Lord & Taylor's famous flagship location in Manhattan into administrative space for some of its growing workforce; the online giant also initiated plans to turn J.C. Penney and Sears stores into distribution warehouses.

In Los Angeles, Hollywood & Highland, a large entertainment complex near the site of the Academy Award ceremonies, was slated to convert 100-thousand square feet of retail space into studios for creative entrepreneurs, as well as reinvent an additional 40-thousand square feet as event space.

In addition, developers across the country were reported to be eyeing hotels whose occupancy rates had crashed during the pandemic, as locations for continuing care retirement communities.

According to Sheila Botting of Avison Young, a Toronto-based commercial real estate firm, in her business "nobody ever lets a crisis get in the way of opportunity."

> "My favorite clients have always been those who are already on to their next idea. This is the American way."
> -Kimberly Ross Clayson, Detroit Business Attorney

From YouTube Viewer to Trend Setter

It's not only big time players who see openings in times of crisis — everyday people do, as well.

A month into the pandemic, for instance, Raymond Cabrera lost a handful of part time jobs that were helping him pay his tuition, rent and car payments during his junior year at Texas State University.

While watching a *Bon Appetit* Magazine "Gourmet Makes" video on YouTube, the 23-year-old was inspired to reinvent himself as a home-based chef and food entrepreneur, in an effort to recoup the earnings he had lost.

Said Raymond, who'd previously considered himself only slightly skilled in the kitchen: "I'm one of those people who needs to work because I have a lot of passion."

He put that passion into creating a unique personal brand of instant ramen—featuring homemade broth, spices and uncooked noodles—which he began packaging in plastic containers and selling to local coffee shops, including one where he'd previously been employed as a barista.

Next, branching out from his initial success, and with an eye toward pandemic-shaken customers, Raymond began cooking up CBD-infused cookies and brownies, which he sold for up to $10 apiece.

Just a few months after Raymond moved into this line of business, it's worth noting that the grand doyenne of all-things-fashionable, Martha Stewart, revamped her own generally conservative product line with the introduction of CBD-based tincture oils and gummies.

Sharing her new creations with a member of the news media, she remarked: "I pop 20 of them and feel just okay, but some of my friends do two and feel high. It's a CBD high, like, relaxed."

> "In order to come back stronger, companies should reinvent their business model. The moment is not to be lost."
> -Kevin Sneader, Managing Partner, McKinsey & Company

And finally……..

We began this chapter with the story of Gabrielle Hamilton, the New York restauranteur who, after being forced to shut down her popular bistro, sat at an empty table and wrote that, despite the gloominess surrounding her, she had begun "dreaming again" of a brighter tomorrow.

At about the same time, across the country, in the mission district of San Francisco, D'Arcy Drollinger resolved to take his dream out into the street.

As owner of the Oasis cabaret, he had long employed a staff of drag queens and kings who performed lampoons of shows like "Sex and the City," and "Buffy the Vampire Slayer" before enthusiastic audiences.

When the virus started to spread, D'Arcy needed to let his employees go—until one day, three months into the COVID-19 crisis, he awoke with a better idea: with closed-down restaurants now surviving by delivering meals to sheltered-in-place customers, *what if* he applied his own creative spin to the delivery concept?

How about delivering dinner, drinks, and a drag show?

Soon after, he asked his performers to "dust off their wigs and heels" and help him launch a new *"Meals on Heels"* service, designed to generate smiles and giggles in an otherwise disheartening time.

Reported a journalist who followed the story:

> *That's how David Landis, the chief executive of a PR firm, found himself watching a drag performer named Poly Poptart as she delivered dinner to his house.*

She strutted up and down the steeply sloped sidewalk outside his home in the Pacific Heights neighborhood, slid down his banister and even did a backflip – in heels, of course.

The performance, Landis said, lifted him out of his pandemic funk. 'I've been a little depressed about this whole Covid thing,' he said, 'but the drag show just brightened my spirits.'

While delivering a laugh or stress relief in times of crisis may not seem comparable, at first blush, to designing outdoor classrooms or urban reinventions, the question of impact is not always clear cut.

Keep in mind that Walt Disney's creation of Mickey Mouse (see Chapter Two) was directly credited with boosting America's recovery, by generating new joy and economic activity in the depths of the Great Depression.

When all is said and done, you never know what an act of crucial creativity might ultimately accomplish.

CHAPTER TEN

Now It's Your Turn

Assessing the destruction left behind in the aftermath of World War II, Winston Churchill urged global leaders to seize the moment, by framing the opportunity in these words:

> *"Never Waste a Good Crisis."*

Through the stories, examples and interviews in this book we have met savvy business leaders, entrepreneurs and career professionals who, facing a broad spectrum of crises, have taken this advice to heart.

And we've studied the strategy — *The Three Acts of Crucial Creativity* — through which they have turned bad news, failures and setbacks into openings for reinvention and long term growth.

In this chapter, we'll convert this proven formula into a user-friendly framework for you to work with as you contemplate, and pursue, your own acts of crucial creativity.

This framework is structured around three key questions:

Question #1
OBSERVATION

What have I observed that has provided me with ideas, opportunities, information or inspiration for crucial creativity?

Question #2
IMAGINEERING

What can I imagine that would transform my observations into solutions, improvements, innovations or inventions?

Question #3
ACTUALIZATION

What skills or abilities would I love to use or develop to turn what I've imagined into reality?

Before you begin working on your personal framework, take a moment to examine, on the following page, how these questions shaped the way forward for Adam Bienenstock, the entrepreneur we met in the previous chapter, as he and his company stared down the prospect of financial disaster during the COVID-19 crisis.

Adam Bienenstock's Crucial Creativity

Crisis Faced: COVID-19 Financial Impact

OBSERVE
Adam observed that the fast-growing COVID-19 case numbers in China would soon spell trouble worldwide for companies, like his, whose customers included schools and childcare centers.

IMAGINEER
Adam and his team reengineered their core playground equipment products into outdoor classrooms designed to help protect students from the spread of the coronavirus.

ACTUALIZE
Adam and his team leveraged their skills and passion for creative manufacturing in order to bring their just-in-time products to market.

OUTCOME
The successful launch of *OutClass*, a new line of outdoor classroom equipment that was designed and manufactured to help protect students and teachers from the spread of COVID-19.

Remember, also, that we saw a number of other examples of applied crucial creativity mapped out in this format—including the reinventive acts of Walt Disney, Jack Conte, Rita Spina and Gil Garcetti—earlier in the book.

Take a look back at these case studies, as well, as you design your own action plan.

Now Is the Time to Begin

While you've been reading this book, no doubt you've been seriously pondering the business or career inventions, or reinventions, you need or want to pursue.

Crucial creativity, as we've seen, entails a series of verbs—steps necessary to achieve success.

So, to help guide your thinking and actions as you move forward, the templates provided on the next several pages, like empty canvases, are waiting for you to fill in their blanks, by prompting you to:

Observe the conditions or circumstances that currently exist, in an exploration for ideas, opportunities, information and inspiration with which to begin the crucial creativity process.

Imagineer (imagine) ways that you might transform your observations into solutions, improvements, innovations or inventions that will meet your needs and the evolving demands of the marketplace.

Remember to ask yourself: *What If?*

Actualize what you've imagined by using the skills and abilities that you identified in your *Personal Inventory* on page 116. If you didn't previously complete your inventory of skills and abilities, take a few moments to go back and do this now.

A Final Note

Please don't hesitate to make copies of the frameworks ahead, or rework your entries as your circumstances or plans continue to develop.

Revisions are to be expected — when we're engaged in the acts of problem-solving, innovation and reinvention, new calculations and changes of heart come with the territory.

And while my hope, going forward, is that you encounter as few crises as possible in your life, business or career, my wish is that your inborn creativity, empowered by the strategy in this book, will bring you enduringly positive results.

My Framework for Crucial Creativity

(Fill in the Blank Boxes)

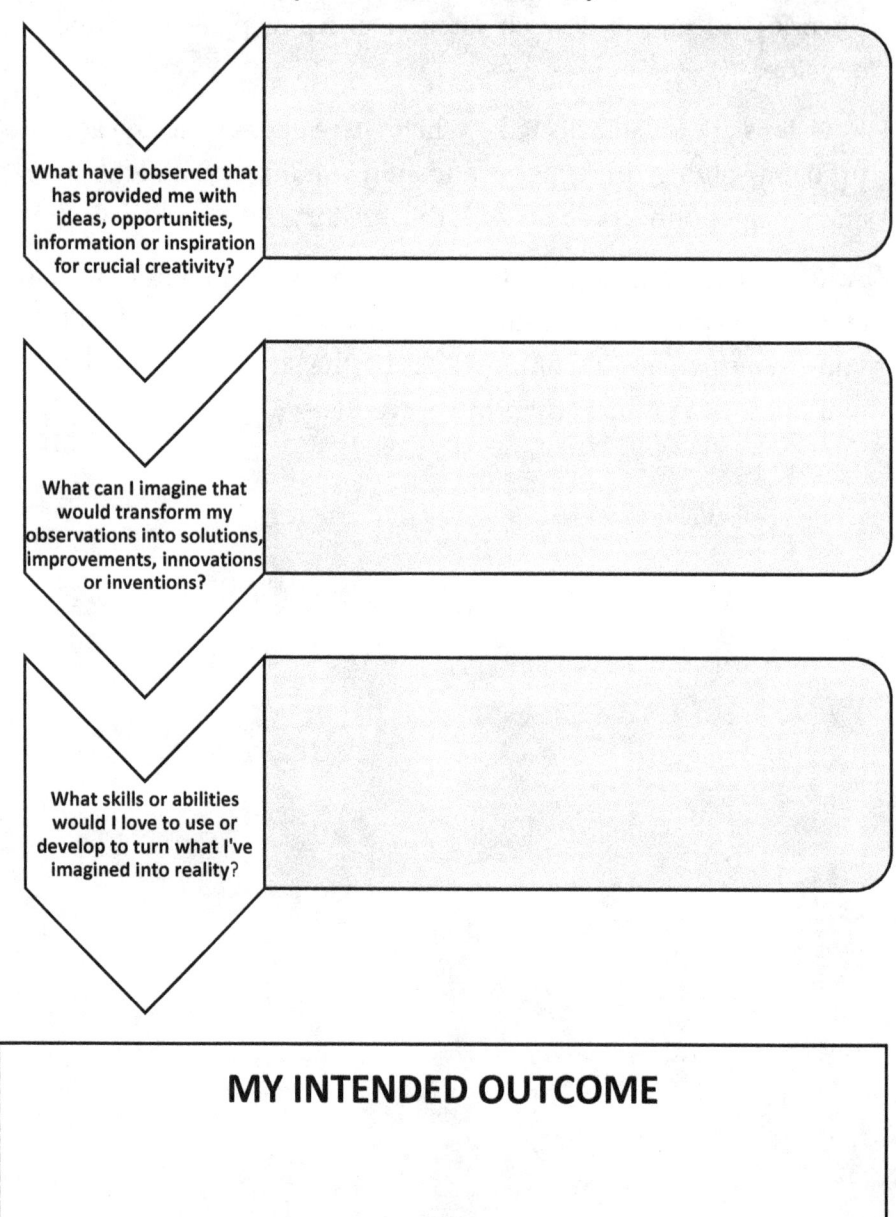

What have I observed that has provided me with ideas, opportunities, information or inspiration for crucial creativity?

What can I imagine that would transform my observations into solutions, improvements, innovations or inventions?

What skills or abilities would I love to use or develop to turn what I've imagined into reality?

MY INTENDED OUTCOME

Now It's Your Turn

My Framework for Crucial Creativity

(Fill in the Blank Boxes)

What have I observed that has provided me with ideas, opportunities, information or inspiration for crucial creativity?

What can I imagine that would transform my observations into solutions, improvements, innovations or inventions?

What skills or abilities would I love to use or develop to turn what I've imagined into reality?

MY INTENDED OUTCOME

Endnotes

Chapter One

There was one day: Drew Dalzell in *Marketplace* interview on National Public Radio, March 26, 2020.

In good times: Jay Rao quoted by Elizabeth Atwater, "Why Do Innovation and Creativity Thrive in Crisis," www.entrepreneurship.babson.edu, April 21, 2020.

Recessions can lead: Dan Priestley, "Why Recession Can Lead to Reinvention," www.entrepreneur.com, March 13, 2020.

It was urgent: Seth Herschthal in personal interviews with the author.

Every creative journey: Jonah Lehrer, *Imagine: How Creativity Works* (Boston: Houghton Mifflin Harcourt, 2012) p.6.

Chapter Two

Where Walt Found: Robin Seaton Jefferson, "Inside Walt Disney's Life in Marceline," Missourilife.com, October 23, 2017.

I drew whatever: Robin Seaton Jefferson, op.cit.

There were actually three: Mark McGuiness, "The Secret of Walt Disney's Creativity," www.lateralaction.com.

The public and: Walt Disney quoted on www.libquotes.com

Mickey Mouse became: wdisneyculturaltransformation.weebly.com.

Chapter Three

Right after graduating: Jack Conte quoted in "Founder's Stories," www.medium.com, December 20, 2018.

I was putting: Jack Conte in personal interview with the author.

Chapter Four

There's no such: Jonah Lehrer, op.cit. p.69

If you find: Robert Sapolsky, "The 2% Difference," *Discover Magazine*, April 4, 2006.

You see a child: Erik Erickson quoted by Scott Barry Kaufman and Carolyn Gregoire, *Wired to Create* (New York, Perigree), 2015, p.3

You come out of college: Sherwin Nuland in personal interviews with the author.

When we tell: Jonah Lehrer, op cit., p.6

Chapter Five

I was trying to: Compilation of Interviews with Eileen Fisher, *New York Times*, October 5, 2018 (David Gelles) *New Yorker Magazine*, September 23, 2013 (Janet Malcolm) *Inc. Magazine*, November 1, 2010.

The faculty of creating: Igor Stravinsky, *The Poetics of Music in Six Lessons* (Cambridge: Harvard University Press, 1947) pp 54-55.

Some inventions could:
Pagan Kennedy, *Inventology: How We Dream Up Things that Change the World* (Boston: Mariner Books, 2016) p.48.

ENDNOTES

Offers meals at approximately: "Chef Davide Oldani and Ristorante D'O." *Harvard Business Review*, January 2013.

It's full of rice fields here: Davide Oldani interviewed in "How the World's Best Chefs Find Inspiration," Oct 25, 2013 blog, www.finedininglovers.com.

It was gnocchi: Davide Oldani interviewed by www.loveitalianlife.com.

I emulated Buddy Holly: Paul McCartney quoted by Austin Kleon, *Steal Like An Artist* (Workman Publishing, 2012), p. 35.

All my songs: Bob Dylan quoted by David Browne, "How Bob Dylan Made a Pre-Rock Masterpiece with Love and Hell," *Rolling Stone Magazine*, September, 2016.

It certainly wasn't big: "Where It All Began: The 1959 Toyopet Crown Custom Sedan" www.autoweek.com, June 6, 2013.

Barring satellite problems: Ted Turner in CNN launch speech, June 1, 1980. www.theverge.com/2015/1/5/7494947/cnn-final-broadcast-doomsday-video.

It's the same story: Sam Elliot in A Star is Born (2018) "Sam Elliot: Bobby," www.ombd.com.

I just had all: Bradley Cooper quoted by Katherine Schaffstall, "Why Bradley Cooper Wanted to Remake A Star is Born," www.hollywoodreporter.com, October 4, 2018

A talented girl: Joe Lynch "Every Version of A Star is Born Ranked Worst to Best," www.billboard.com, October 4, 2018.

Perhaps the next: Rebecca Keegan, "Why Every Era Gets the A Star Is Born It Deserves," www.vanityfair.com, October, 2018.

One of the finest: Gene Weingarten, "Pearls Before Breakfast," *Washington Post*, April 8, 2007.

I noticed that: Kevin Roose, "How I Ditched My Phone and Unbroke My Brain," *New York Times*, February 23, 2019.

Chapter Six

Creators have a vested interest: Fredrich Wilhelm Nietzche quoted by Mario Popova in "How Creativity Works from Nietzche to Johan Lehrer," *The Atlantic*, March 22, 2012.

One of the greatest problems: Eugene Kwon M.D., **So the hypothesis**: Val Lowe M.D., quoted in "Mayo Clinic Gets Approval for New Prostate Cancer Drug," *Forefront Magazine*, Volume 2, Issue 1, 2013, www.mayo.edu.

What is imagination: Frank Wilczek,"What is the value of Imagination and Wishful Thinking in Science?," July 17, 2017, www.bigquestionsonline.com.

When I get: Nickola Tesla quoted by Thomas Oppong in "Daily routines of Nikola Tesla, et al," February 7, 2017, www.cnbc.com.

When you ask: Steve Jobs quoted by Derek Doepker in "Steve Jobs Systematically Cultivated His Creativity, You Can Too," *Entrepreneur Magazine*, August 3, 2017.

E.T. was never: Steven Spielberg, interview video and online transcripts, www/syfy.com.

When I placed: Mary Shelley quoted by Greg Buzwell, "Mary Shelly, Frankenstein and the Villa Diodati," *British Library Collection*, May 15, 2014, www.bl.uk.

I woke up: Paul McCartney, *Beatles Anthology* (San Francisco: Chronicle Books, 2000) p. 175.

Endnotes

This is secret: Salvador Dali, *50 Secrets of Master Craftsmanship* (New York: Dover Publications, 1992) p. 36.

Letting your mind: Jonathan Schooler quoted by Jonah Lehrer in *Imagine: How Creativity Works* (Boston: Houghton Mifflin Harcourt, 2012) p.48-9.

You need a quiet: Eric Maisel PhD, *Fearless Creating* (New York: Jeremy Tarcher/Putnam, 1995) pp 4,5,6.

On his walk: Walter Isaacson, *Albert Einstein: His Life and Universe* (New York, Simon & Schuster, 2007) pp 438-9.

Chapter Seven

You've got to find: Steve Jobs, Stanford University Commencement Address, www.stanford.edu, June 12, 2005.

My three year stint: Justin Shane, "I Was a Lawyer, Then I Found My Calling in the basement of a Mexican Restaurant," *New York Times*, October 5, 2018.

Whatever happens: Marion Rosen in personal interview with the author.

Creative persons differ: Mihaly Csikszentmihalyi, *Creativity: Flow and the Psychology of Discovery and Invention* (New York, Harper Perennial, 1997) p.107.

You have an idea: Joshua Roth quoted by Thessaly La Force, *New York Times Style Magazine*, February 25, 2019.

It gives me: Sherwin B. Nuland in personal interview with the author.

We found the same: Mihaly Csikszentmihalyi, op.cit. pp. 106, 11.

Chapter Eight

And I went: Rita K. Spina in personal interview with the author.

Of course we do: Michael Merzenich in personal interview with the author.

The day after: Gil Garcetti in personal interview with the author.

Chapter Nine

I, like hundreds: Gabrielle Hamilton, "The Kitchen is Closed," *New York Times Magazine*, April 26, 2020, p. 61

I was looking: John Bienenstock in personal interview with the author.

The backbone: John Kapon quoted by Paul Sullivan, "Open to New Ideas in a Shutdown," *New York Times*, April 18, 2020, p. B7.

Nobody ever lets: Sheila Botting quoted by Tom Citelli, "Empty Space Becomes a Blank Canvas," *New York Times*, September 2, 2020, p. B6.

I'm one of:
Raymond Cabrera quoted by Allyson Waller, "College Students are Getting Creative as Traditional Jobs Disappear," *New York Times*, August 26, 2020, p. A7.

I pop 20: Martha Stewart quoted by Sheila Mariker, "Here's How You Do It," *New York Times*, September 17, 2020, p. D1.

That's how David: Concepcion de Leon, "They've Got Fierce Moves, and Your Dinner," *New York Times*, September 11, 2020, p. A14.

Author's Note: The author's personal interviews with individuals and subject experts in this book have been lightly edited and condensed for clarity and flow.

Acknowledgments

This book is the result of crucial creativity brought to life through the generous assistance of others.

In March of 2020, when the coronavirus first struck the U.S. in earnest, I had just completed work on a different sort of book — one focused on the growth of a new widespread hunger for creative expression and accomplishment — a happening characterized by some as a global 'creativity boom.'

A month later, after the virus crashed the U.S. publishing industry, disrupting the release of that book and hundreds more by other authors, it abruptly became apparent that creativity was more than a timely topic — it was a crucial need.

What If? I asked myself, I reinvented the book I had recently completed, for the purpose of transforming it into a strategic guide to creativity for business owners, corporate executives, and career professionals whose lives had been upended by the COVID crisis — or might one day face crises of other kinds?

Accomplishing this, I believed, might empower readers to think and act more creatively whenever tough times came their way — as Winston Churchill put it, to "never let a good crisis go to waste."

Transforming this book from an idea into reality would not have been possible without the in-depth interviews granted to me by Seth Herschthal, owner of Blue Star Camps in Hendersonville, N.C., John Bienenstock, CEO of Bienenstock Natural Playgrounds, based outside Toronto, and Jack Conte, co-founder and CEO of Patreon.com.

I am in their debt for providing me with real-life case studies and first person insights into the process of surviving and thriving when best-laid plans strike an unforeseen iceberg.

Others to whom I owe a similar gratitude include Gil Garcetti, former District Attorney of Los Angeles, Michael Merzenich, the pioneering neuroscientist who discovered the 'brain plasticity' phenomenon.

It's imperative that I add a shout out to Mark Miller, my friend, colleague and fellow journalist, who was kind enough to write the foreword to this book, and whose writings and podcasts provide creative, plain language financial 'news you can use' to an eager audience each day.

At Profit Research, Inc., I benefited greatly from the publishing expertise of Marjorie Marks and her outstanding team. And certainly not to be forgotten are Tracy Atkins, my book designer, and Tanja Prokop, our cover designer—they have my appreciation for a job well done, as does Claire McKinney, who literally wrote the book on the way great publicists operate.

Each time I've embarked on an ambitious writing adventure like this one, I have done so knowing that I am supported by one of the best 'managing editors' I've ever known—my wife, Jane. Whenever I felt like I couldn't stand to revise one more line, or clarify another concept, she always gently nudged me forward to a better result.

To Jane and to my father, the late Sidney Walton—writer, broadcast pioneer, and publisher extraordinaire—I extend my deepest appreciation for always being my north stars.

About the Author

A Life of Reinvention

Mark S. Walton is a Peabody award-winning broadcast journalist, Fortune 100 management consultant, educational entrepreneur, and nonfiction author whose work focuses on leadership and exceptional achievement in life, work and business.

He has been a Professor of Leadership in the U.S. Navy's Advanced Management Program, at the top-ranked Senior Executive Institute and Kenan-Flagler Graduate Business School at the University of North Carolina-Chapel Hill, and at Toyota University.

In his role as Chairman of the *Center for Leadership Communication*, which he founded in 1995, Mark has taught, coached, advised and spoken to thousands of leaders, managers and talented professionals in executive programs at many of the world's leading organizations including: Bank of America, Dow Chemical, General Electric Corporation, Duke Energy, Glaxo SmithKline, NASA, and the United States Navy and Marine Corps.

In addition to *Crucial Creativity*, he is the author of *Boundless Potential: Transform Your Brain, Unleash Your Talents, Reinvent Your Work in Midlife and Beyond,* which became the focus of a 90-minute nationwide PBS Network Television Special. His previous book, *Generating Buy-In: Mastering the Language of Leadership*, was selected as one of the year's top 30 business books by Soundview Executive Summaries.

Earlier in his career, Mark was CNN's first Chief White House Correspondent and later CNN Senior Correspondent and Anchorman, traveling the globe from network headquarters in Atlanta. He is a recipient of broadcast journalism's premier honor, the George Foster Peabody Award, for his role in CNN's live coverage of the failed 1991 Soviet coup, and the subsequent fall of Communism.

His research, writing and reporting on business leadership and career achievement, as well as on major social trends and issues, have been honored with the National Headliner Award, Ohio State Journalism Award, Cable Ace Award, Gold Medal of the New York TV and Film Festival and the Silver Gavel of the American Bar Association.

To send your thoughts and comments on this book, or share your own stories about business, career or personal reinvention, Mark can be reached by email through his corporate website at www.leadercommunication.com.

Also by Mark S. Walton

Boundless Potential: Transform Your Brain, Unleash Your Talents, Reinvent Your Work in Midlife and Beyond

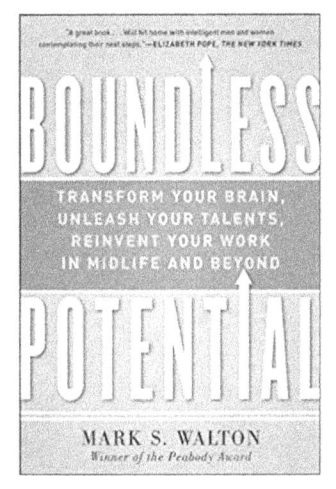

What is the lifelong potential of the human mind?

Might I have talents or brainpower that I'm not aware of?

Can I make money and a difference doing something I love?

Is there some science to this or just luck?

Personally driven by these questions, Peabody award-winning journalist and Fortune 100 leadership consultant Mark S. Walton set out on his most fascinating assignment yet.

Crisscrossing America to meet with remarkably re-inventive people, and researching the latest breakthroughs in brain science, creativity and happiness, he made three life-altering discoveries:

State-of-the-art neuroscience has revealed that we are hard-wired for reinvention through the emergence of extraordinary new brainpowers in life's second half.

A growing number of men and women are learning to leverage this inborn potential. In midlife, they're raising the bar — inventing profitable new careers, businesses, and avenues for social impact that extend well into their 70's, 80's, even 90's.

Longevity experts are increasingly convinced that doing work that 'pays it forward' to future generations pays us back in personal long-term health and happiness.

In *Boundless Potential*, Walton explores these surprising and encouraging findings, weaving first-hand accounts, cutting edge research, and practical lessons into an actionable blueprint for redesigning our lives and work.

"A wonderful guide. *Boundless Potential* explores the science of lifelong potential and explains how individuals can create work they love. An inspiring read."

— Glenn Ruffenach, *Wall Street Journal*

"A great book. The mix of history, psychology, neuroscience and profiles of successful re-inventers will hit home with intelligent men and women contemplating their next steps."

— Elizabeth Pope, *The New York Times*

"A terrific book. *Boundless Potential* provides clear and practical advice on how to navigate the transition from work to good work; and if that isn't enough, Mark Walton is a master storyteller."

— Suzanne Braun Levine, *Founding Editor, Ms. Magazine*

Also by Mark S. Walton

Generating Buy-In: Mastering the Language of Leadership

In the workplace, marketplace and public arena, the ability to generate buy-in, to influence people's thoughts and feelings, has become the #1 leadership skill.

Generating Buy-In imparts a simple and actionable approach to even the most complex leadership, management, sales or marketing challenges – it will empower you to:

- *Design a strategic story that projects a positive future to your audience.*
- *Speak the language of buy-in with images that mold people's thoughts and emotions.*
- *Put this language to work, whether your goal is to inspire an audience, lead a team, raise sales or win an election.*

In this short, potent book, Mark S. Walton, Fortune 100 leadership consultant and former CNN Chief White House Correspondent, will show you how to design and implement the communication methodology used by leaders such as General Electric's Jack Welch, Intel's Andy Grove, President Ronald Reagan and even Winston Churchill.

Complete with examples, practical exercises, sample business scenarios, and a Foreword by William Ury PhD, coauthor of the international best-seller *Getting to Yes*.

Selected as one of the year's top 30 business books by Soundview Executive Summaries, *Generating Buy-In* is an indispensable resource for leading and succeeding in today's fiercely competitive world!

"Anyone interested in influencing fellow human beings can benefit from this book's wise and practical advice. It's a keeper!"

— William Ury PhD, bestselling coauthor, *Getting to Yes*

"This book unlocks secrets top leaders have applied through the ages. Instinctively you know that Mark Walton has hit the bulls-eye, because it feels right in your heart and your gut. Wonderfully simple and effective!"

— Ron Kirkpatrick, National Manager, Toyota Motor Sales, USA

"*Generating Buy-In* is a must read. Walton applies timeless wisdom to today's business world and, most importantly, shows how to take action. You will be a more effective leader if you follow the steps in this book"

— Frank T. Morgan PhD, Global Director of Leadership Development, Dow Chemical

CPSIA information can be obtained
at www.ICGtesting.com
Printed in the USA
LVHW030717180121
676771LV00003B/163